Jackie Bennett started her career in theatre production before moving into television and writing. From 1987 to 1993 she co-produced several documentary series with Rosemary Forgan including *There's Something About a Convent Girl* (Bamboo Productions/ITV, 1991) on which this book was based. She studied history and garden design and is the author of several books including *Wild About the Garden*.

Rosemary Forgan, after spending her entire primary and secondary school years in the care of various orders of nuns, escaped to the secular world of film and television, firstly working for Orson Welles and then in the news and current affairs department of Thames Television. In 1987 she set up Bamboo Film & Television Productions with Jackie Bennett and has since produced a number of television documentaries and series. Besides *There's Something About a Convent Girl* for ITV, these include *Gardeners' World* for BBC/Catalyst, *Where Were You?* for ITV and *The Lost Gardens of Heligan* a Bamboo/ Cicada co-production for Channel Four. In addition, she writes for a number of newspapers and magazines on subjects as varied as travel, interior design and property.

CONVENT GIRLS

Edited by

JACKIE BENNETT *and*

ROSEMARY FORGAN

Virago

A *Virago* Book

This edition published by Virago Press 2003

First published by Virago Press Limited 1991

This collection, Introduction, A Short History
and After Vatican II copyright © Jackie Bennett
and Rosemary Forgan 1991

Copyright © in each contribution held by the author

The rights of Jackie Bennett and Rosemary Forgan to be identified as
editors of this work have been asserted by them in accordance with the
Copyright, Designs and Patents Act 1988.

A CIP catalogue record for this title
is available from the British Library

ISBN 1 84408 099 4

Typeset in Baskerville by M Rules
Printed and bound in Great Britain
by Clays Ltd, St Ives plc.

Virago Press
An imprint of
Time Warner Books UK
Brettenham House
Lancaster Place
London
WC2E 7EN

www.virago.co.uk

Contents

Acknowledgements

Our thanks are due to many Catholic girls – and boys – who gave so generously of their time to share their individual experiences of convent schooldays, and particularly for allowing us to use edited transcripts of the interviews in this book. Thanks to Miss Helen Mabey, Penny, Claire and Ann for making life at Gumley House bearable and even, occasionally, great fun. Thanks to Sue Street, who received a crash course on Catholicism while typing endless hours of transcripts, Mandy Little for her observation and encouragement while reading endless reams of transcripts and Roger Bolton formerly of Thames Television for having faith in the project in the first place.

Foreword

When this book was first published in 1991 it opened with two quotes from authors writing fifty years apart, talking about events which happened 100 years apart, but thus neatly illustrating a key point: that the experience of a convent education just did not change. The memories of girls educated in Australia in the 1950s matched uncannily those of girls who went to school in England in the 1920s – or the 1960s. In a changing world it seemed this at least would always stay the same. And then, dramatically, it changed beyond all recognition.

In 1964 there were some 5,000 teaching nuns in the UK alone. By 1990 this had dropped by 80% to around 1,000. In 2001 (the last year for which figures are currently available) there were just 252. Such a dramatic decline in any other 'endangered species' would have made headline news but this particular near-extinction almost seems to have gone unnoticed.

Even when the first edition of this book came out, the winds of change, post-Vatican II, had brought about differences. Girls like Mary O'Hara (then an undergraduate, now a *Guardian* reporter) had experienced a far less authoritarian regime than older 'girls'. But a Catholic education without nuns? The idea was unthinkable – yet that is precisely what has happened.

Ms Oona Stannard, Director of the Catholic Education Service takes an optimistic view, that somehow 'the essence' of the nuns (their influence, their tradition, their devotion) still lingers and serves to make a Catholic education different from any other. It is almost a 'homeopathic' view, that no matter how much something is diluted, the efficacy remains. Professor Gerald Grace, Director of the Centre for Research and Development in Catholic Education, fears the worst in that whilst most Catholic schools today employ teachers who were themselves educated by nuns or priests, soon this influence will disappear completely. He fears the 'spiritual capital' which made Catholic schools special will then be lost.

Who knows which view will prove correct? But this book, which started out as a contemporary look at an education system that formed and forged some of the most independent and successful women of the twentieth century, has become, somewhat unexpectedly, an eye-witness record of what is now a little piece of history.

Rosemary Forgan

Introduction

'What I really liked about *Eve* was that after the play went out
I had masses of letters from girls all over Britain, all convinced
that I had modelled it on their old school . . .'

Marcella Evaristi, playwright
Eve Set The Balls of Corruption Rolling, BBC TV play, 1984

'Soon after my book *Frost in May* appeared, I received two
letters from "old children" of Lippington. One of the writers
had left in 1883; the other in 1927; both were quite certain
from my description of the convent, that I must have been
their contemporary. The fact I left in 1914 is irrelevant.'

Antonia White, author *Frost in May*, 1933

The things you hear, or indeed remember from personal
experience, about convent education may strike you as
bizarre, inspiring or brutal, according to one's stand on
these matters, but what is quite breathtaking to most people
is the similarity of the experience.

Unlikely as it sounds, it was as if women in religious
orders, not just in Britain but all over the *world*, conspired to
produce an identical female educational system that hardly
changed by so much as a comma in 150 years. For decades
the bird's eye view (if They were watching from Above)
must have been of nuns busying about in every corner of

the globe, worrying and fussing over girls' hem-lines, urging that unpalatable food be offered up for the souls in Purgatory, making sure their little charges were word perfect on the Catechism and, most important of all, alerting them to the perils lurking in wait in that sin-sodden place, The Outside World.

Authors Germaine Greer and Maeve Binchy were educated by nuns at the opposite ends of the earth, yet both recall leaving school believing, in Maeve's words, 'that the world was going to be full of lovely pulsating, steaming lust'.

In reality we know the nuns were too busy to spend much time pooling information even within the same Order, much less outside of it, so it is all the more extraordinary that women educated in Melbourne, Bombay, New York and Dublin, with names and personalities as diverse as President Cory Aquino, Marianne Faithful, Benazir Bhutto and Lady Antonia Fraser are as much united by similar memories of their schooldays as they are separated by years or the continents that divide them.

Each time Mary O'Malley's hugely successful play *Once a Catholic* is revived, at the interval the only sound to be heard in the theatre bar, apart from the chink of glasses, is middle-aged and older women exclaiming: 'But that was *just* like the Sacred Heart ...' or 'I'm sure they modelled that nun on Mother Perpetua ...'

The other thing that strikes a lot of people is how, with all that emphasis on humility, modesty and the putting of almost everybody before oneself, the nuns managed to produce so many extraordinarily strong-minded women. 'Bloody-minded' is how the nuns would probably have described them, had they ever resorted to such phraseology. Yet, ironically, without that particular character trait, be it vice or virtue, it is doubtful that many of the original founders of religious orders would actually have got their projects off the ground in the first place – given their battles with Rome, with Protestants, and with men in general who often took a very dim view of the whole idea.

Myths

> 'Our Lady has promised that Ireland will sink beneath the waves seven years before the end of the world, in order that the Irish be spared all the awful things that will be happening.'

So we were told, hand on heart, at my grammar school. Unfortunately, my genuinely innocent enquiry as to (a) why seven years? and (b) what would happen to all the Irish people living in New York, Birmingham, Liverpool, Kilburn, etc., was interpreted as 'veiled insolence', and the remainder of the lesson was spent standing outside in the corridor – so alas I never did find out the answer!

Myths become second nature to the convent girl, particularly if she has been educated by one of the many orders of Irish nuns who were always happy to interweave their extraordinarily imaginative folklore with Catholic dogma.

Some of the other myths we were told now seem curiously out of date. Like the warning about the sinful woman (a 'non-Catholic' of course) who went up to the altar and took the Host, returned to her seat, took it out of her mouth and transferred it to her handkerchief. Nowadays Catholics have the option of opening their mouths or putting out their hand to receive the Holy Sacrament but in those days the very idea of anyone but the priest actually touching the Host was totally shocking. No one was thus surprised to hear that on later examination the Host in the hankie had miraculously been transformed into a small pool of blood. It is only in retrospect that it seems rather sad that the nuns felt obliged to confuse this potentially beautiful ritual with such frightening warnings and negative imagery. The nuns were quite shameless when it came to using 'The Myth' to scare and/or coax their charges into good behaviour:

'Our Lady blushes every time you cross your legs' was a frequent admonition. One wonders what she must now be making of all those 'new wave' nuns, wearing their Marks and Spencer skirts – and crossing their legs unashamedly! Of course there comes a point for most Catholic girls when myths have to be tested:

> 'It was only when I went to University that I dared *not* to go to Mass on Sunday. I remember I lay in bed all day, waiting for something terrible to happen. I was really quite surprised when it got to seven o'clock in the evening – without the ceiling having fallen in or some other catastrophe – I seemed to "have got away with it". No one could have been more surprised.'
>
> Ann Burns, TV director

Perhaps because it is a relatively small step, the convent girl seems to make an easy transition from *believing* myths to becoming one herself. As Marina Warner puts it:

'I don't really understand how the myth of the sexy convent
girl grew up. But then again it does so often turn out that the
girl dancing naked on top of the piano at the party *did* go to a
convent school . . .'

The well-behaved young lady, attending her convent
school, was for a long time the popular parental fantasy.
Strangely it sat side by side with the adolescent boys' fantasy
about the raver-nymphomaniac who looked as if butter
wouldn't melt in her mouth. When Marianne Faithful
arrived on the scene in the early 60s she fitted the bill beautifully as the archetypal dream-convent-girl. 'Bambi with a
migrained face' is how author John Walsh now describes
her, but in those days, with her modest Peter Pan collar and
long skirts, she looked like a teenage cherub with just a
hint of something terribly naughty lurking below the sur-
face. Something the nuns usually described as 'bold'.

A rather more earthy saying, also of the time, was, 'Show
me a girl wearing a cross round her neck and I'll show you
a dead cert!'

It is perhaps interesting to note that it is almost impossible to talk to 'old convent girls' (roughly those between
thirty and ninety) without sex coming into the conversation
as far as school memories are concerned. The constant
admonition '*not to*' seems to have worked in reverse, turning
it into a major preoccupation. Interestingly, the 'new' convent girls, though curious as young girls always will be, seem
to place the whole matter a lot further down the agenda of
important things to worry about. Again, it is only looking
back that it seems an exceptionally odd idea to leave the sex

education of adolescent girls in the hands of women who presumably had absolutely no first-hand knowledge of the subject at all. Yet what the nuns lacked in hands-on experience, to use an unfortunate phrase, they certainly made up for in imagination. Little did they realise that to some extent it had the opposite effect, sharpening curiosity where none hitherto existed.

The wholly unacceptable face of convent 'modesty' is perhaps best demonstrated by Deirdre McSharry, once British editor of *Cosmopolitan* magazine. She recalls her days at a convent in Ireland during the war years when the fixation with purity was so strong that pupils weren't even supposed to see their own bodies, never mind anyone else's, even when getting washed:

'On bath night we all had to put on a sort of knitted bathing costume before we got into the bath to wash . . .'

That sounds bad enough but worse was yet to come: 'The bad news was that there was just the one, soggy costume we all had to take turns to share.'

Bells and Smells

One of the areas that almost everybody did seem to like about their convent experience was the bombardment of the senses provided by their everyday surroundings. The correct term is probably sensual pleasures – but few girls would feel comfortable with that phrase when describing conditions *inside* the convent, any convent!

But they were pleasures of the senses certainly, and sadly,

ones that today's bright-eyed, bushy-tailed girls will probably miss out on.

The first impression for almost everybody was the 'whooshing' of black serge skirts. Full enough to bury your face in as a tiny child, one became increasingly grateful, as the years went by, for the accompanying clacking rosary beads which signalled a nun's approach. 'Like a rattle-snake's warning' was how one eighty-year-old convent girl described it.

Squeaky rubber-soled shoes on highly polished wooden floors, beeswax and the occasional whiff of incense – all of these seem to rate highly with almost all convent girls, no matter how much they may have hated the rest of the regime, or how far they wandered from the path of Catholicism in later life. However, the real highlight of the year was the May procession – a red-letter day in the convent girl's calendar.

'Bring flowers of the rarest, bring blossoms the fairest, from garden and woodland and hillside and dale . . .' goes the hymn. It could equally well have been describing all those excited little girls, dressed in their Holy Communion frocks, some of them now straining at the seams in places. This was *the* day when the Queen of the May, an older 'trustie' girl, would crown the statue of Our Lady. It was a grand excuse for all the little rituals that make Catholicism a picturesque religion: everyone had white gloves, white sandals, white socks, white hymn book or missal; while the favourite old hymns were sung, those with the elevated title of 'strewer' went ahead, scattering their rose petals in the path of the Queen. Like all halcyon, childhood memories, the ceremony *always* took place on a perfect summer day.

Such was the pull of the May processions that 'non-Catholic' parents whose children attended convent schools frequently became worried their daughters were being seduced by the Papist rituals.

Considering that convent education, in Britain at least, is a minority education, there is no doubt it has produced a disproportionate number of hugely successful women, particularly in the creative world of writing and the media. Whilst some women attribute their success directly to their convent education, others agree there was a link but feel they have succeeded in spite of, rather than because of it.

One of them who feels that certain aspects did help is writer Deirdre McSharry:

> 'I think one of the things that has helped me as a journalist is my awareness of smells – and their contribution to atmosphere. Undoubtedly that does come from my convent days which are full of memories of the smell of incense, of wax, of wood. An appreciation of . . . richness.'

Not all the rituals were exactly jolly though, as Scottish playwright Marcella Evaristi points out about daily Mass:

> 'When you're little it never strikes you as odd – all that fainting, and girls falling down like skittles every morning. It's only afterwards you think, "Hey, do they do that elsewhere – make children stand and pray until they fall over?"'

Something else that only seems odd afterwards was the commonplace practice of teaching children as young as five or six how to baptise a baby in an emergency, using their favourite doll to practise on. 'The need to know' was backed up with the justification that: 'Your mother might have a baby that's very sickly, and your mother might even die, so while everybody else is running around worrying about that, *you* can baptise the baby and save him from Limbo.' Limbo was a sort of annexe of hell, thought not *quite* as unpleasant, where the souls of unbaptised babies were dispatched. Nobody questioned the wisdom of scaring little children out of their wits by suggesting that their mother might not be long for this world.

The bizarre rider to this is that when a friend, who had only heard about this practice fairly recently, expressed his horror my first, split-second reaction was, 'But surely that's preferable to letting the baby go to Limbo.' In fact Limbo has been abolished, although what has become of all those unbaptised babies (and there must be an awful lot of them by now) is not clear.

Gym Slips and Other Odd Habits

There seems little doubt one aspect of convent education that appeals to parents is the idea of a school uniform. In turn the efforts made by offspring to 'liven it up a bit', even 'make it a bit more modern' deserve awards for creativity. Of course such gestures were guaranteed to cause quite a stir. Memories of the battles waged over the wearing of school

uniform seem to linger in most people's memory. Britain's
highest ranking woman police officer, Assistant Chief
Constable Alison Halford, clearly recalls that at her school,
eating in uniform, in the street, 'was almost a capital offence'.
Playwright Mary O'Malley was accused of wearing her uniform 'in a slick way' whatever that might mean!

A great deal of thought went into those adaptations.
Someone at my school worked out that if you wore a very
wide elasticated belt *over* your gym slip or summer dress and
then buttoned up your cardigan, the overall effect was of
tiny waist and shorter flared skirt (all the rage at the time). Of
course it was only a matter of time before one of the nuns,
curiosity aroused no doubt by the sight of a girl wearing a
buttoned-up cardigan in baking heat, decided to investigate.
Nuns seemed to spend a lot of their time like this, sleuthing
around, looking for something wrong – based on no more
than a feeling that *something* was going on. On many occasions, of course, their intuition was absolutely right.

In a convent school there was always an enormous temptation to get involved in at least some minor mischief
because it took so little to reduce the nuns to a state of complete apoplexy. Only the truly compassionate could have
resisted it – and who feels compassion towards their teachers in their teens?

Sins and Sanctions

What really separated the convent school from any other
school, religious or secular, was that they convinced you

they had God on their side – and woe betide anyone who forgot that.

One of the curious anomalies of Roman Catholicism generally is that while the Church tends to view its flock as a set of fairly simple-minded souls, who need very little to distract them from the path of righteousness, there is also the contradictory assumption that quite tiny children *do* understand right from wrong and are capable of handling a very complicated system of 'plea bargaining'. The novenas, the rosaries, the indulgences are all part of this and the penalty for anyone who fails to come up to scratch (and of course unless you are guilty of the sin of pride, you will assume you *don't* come up to scratch) will be a residue of guilt about whatever they do.

The only thing is . . . guilt these days is automatically assumed to be a bad thing, so most people get rid of it. Accidents happen on railways and people get hurt, children are murdered while under the 'supervision' of a social worker, people fail to deliver goods on time or go bankrupt owing millions. But perish the thought they should feel guilty about it – 'It's not *my* fault,' they say. 'Nothing to do with me.' Which is the real dilemma for the Catholic – lapsed or otherwise: Is the guilt just a lingering left-over of early brainwashing or the healthy sign of an active conscience? Answers on a postcard please . . .

So much has changed as far as convent schools are concerned it would probably be difficult for today's convent girls to identify with much of the foregoing. Nowadays their manner, their attitudes, their aspirations and ambitions are virtually unrecognisable to those educated in pre-Vatican II days.

Of the 'new breed' of convent girls few of them seem able to recite the catechism, whilst the majority appear to support the idea that sleeping with a steady boyfriend is the normal thing to do – behaviour that only a generation ago would have been more than enough to justify immediate expulsion *and* have the whole community on their knees, praying for the sinner's soul. At best they also appear to share a very positive attitude to life and their education. For the most part, academic standards at convents have always been high, but these girls appear to have been encouraged in other ways: to question just about every subject under the sun, and they have been treated as adults – rather than potential 'occasions of sin' as were previous generations. The resulting maturity makes them a credit to their educators.

At the risk of sounding perverse, what they haven't had, in these enlightened times, is an education occasionally so insane that one had no choice but to rebel, thus sampling at an early age the heady delights of rebellion! Then again, maybe today's convent education is closer to the ideals of the early founders, enabling children to fulfil their potential free of that heavy burden of guilt.

Rosemary Forgan, 1991

A Short History

When a girl enters a Catholic convent school, at whatever age, she is aware of becoming part of a great tradition stretching back into the depths of history. For a child, it is sometimes difficult to untangle the threads of this awesome tradition and work out her relationship with this past.

The convent girls we interviewed, located as they were in the twentieth century, all spoke of their sense of history; the importance of belonging to an ancient international body – the Catholic Church. Whether they experienced this as an unnecessarily heavy burden or as an enriching and useful intellectual discipline depended very much on their own individual circumstances. The problem for many of them was deciphering the religious facts from the religious fervour. So much of convent teaching was bound up with a particular (Catholic) dogma. Nuns, by virtue of their profession, interpreted the past in terms of their own faith. For English convent girls this was further complicated by the teachings of Irish nuns who had, in many cases, been totally isolated from the outside world and were consequently steeped in superstition. These nuns could only pass on their own version of reality, embroidered with the legends of Irish mythology.

Nevertheless, a Catholic convent schoolgirl of the 1950s was probably better versed in the stories, events, beliefs and characters of her faith than her Protestant counterpart. This was indeed a colourful pageant, beginning with 'Our Lady', the mother of Jesus Christ – just one example (albeit the most important) of a historical figure who attained mythical status. Many girls complained that their historical knowledge was heavily biased, with the Catholics always playing the 'goodies' and conveniently omitting the Spanish Inquisition and other dubious Catholic escapades. There was also great emphasis on the suffering of women; on martyrdom and sainthood; on women who endured agony for the Catholic cause. One such latter-day saint was Maria Goretti, who was held up as an encouragement to all good Catholic girls. She was an Italian peasant girl who, in 1902, resisted rape by a farm labourer and was viciously stabbed to death. No one doubted her bravery, but it was a curious choice of heroine for 'modern girls' who might be about to indulge in 'sinful pleasures' as a Catholic Truth Society pamphlet of the 1950s suggested. It went on to warn its young readers to 'Be pure or perish'.

Yet, from within this sometimes gory collection of stories, a fascinating history does emerge. The nuns often seemed to be the last ones to acknowledge or pass on their own history, or to recount with pride their own traditions of struggle and achievement, particularly in the field of education, hampered as they were by the need to satisfy a higher authority than themselves: the Church and the Pope, who is the vicar of Christ Himself.

It wasn't always so. Since the first centuries after Christ, the first 'Christian centuries', women have left their homes to join religious groups and opt for an alternative to marriage and childbirth. At first only loosely held together by a devotion to communal prayer, in the fourth, fifth and sixth centuries these women (and men) took up a lifestyle which would form the basis of religious life, by committing themselves to fasting and inward contemplation. It was at this time that the Bishop of Arles in France wrote down the Rule for women's orders – that they should give up their property, remain cloistered and celibate, become self-sufficient, spending their days in prayer, study and singing. All over Europe well-born women would give up their jewels and finery to join a nunnery or convent. As early as AD 400 Saint Brigid had set up a community in Kildare, Ireland. It was also the time that Augustine was laying down his philosophy of what a woman's role should be in wider society, as defined by the Church. The first duty of women in marriage should be loyalty and then procreation. Sexual pleasure became 'concupiscence' and any sexual activity outside of marriage became 'fornication'. The only way a woman could rise above her 'sinful' nature was to remain virginal and achieve Christian salvation.

In France and England many of the early 'monasteries' were in fact 'dual houses' for men and women. In Anglo-Saxon England these were invariably ruled by an Abbess. Men and women shared equally in the new Christianity and within these houses, a woman could devote herself entirely to study and prayer – exercising her intellectual and spiritual capacity to an extent just not possible in the outside world. There was no question of these nuns receiving anything other than great respect and admiration from their male counterparts, if only because the Abbesses themselves

had great power over land, over property and over the
monks and nuns in their care.

The best documentated of these Abbesses is Hild of
Northumbria (later canonised St Hilda). She founded the
great abbeys of Whitby and Hartlepool in the seventh century as places of serious Christian education. Her charges
studied and wrote in Latin and under her tuition five men
from Whitby went on to become bishops. Always on the
look-out for new creative talent, she discovered that a lay
worker on her estate called Caedmon sang and composed
the most beautiful poetry. Although he could neither read
nor write she took him into the abbey and harnessed his
talent as a teaching medium for her monks who learnt this
new discipline of Anglo-Saxon poetry from him. Caedmon
is now accepted as the first great Anglo-Saxon poet and his
gift was an invaluable tool for the passing on of Anglo-
Saxon and the subsequent development of the English
language.

By the eighth century there were over twenty monasteries for women in England and a similar number in France
and Belgium. Throughout the continent noble families were
sending their daughters to be educated at these religious
houses – Repton in Derbyshire, Chelles in France and
Gandersheim in Germany – which were fast becoming educational centres of excellence and all headed by an Abbess.
A 'convent life' was established as a viable alternative to
more conventional roles. Royal and noble women queued to
join, bequeathing their lands and their properties as
'dowries' and thus ensuring the financial viability of the
houses. The Abbess would be responsible not only for the

education of the nuns and monks in her care but for the administration of the estate, the collecting of tithes and for appointing village clergy. Their sphere of learning was also expanding to include not only Latin, Anglo-Saxon and religion, but botany and medicine as well – Hildegard of Bingen (1098–1179) in Germany was renowned throughout Europe for her herbals, medical reference books and scientific treatises. Although Hildegard was exceptional, even the average nuns would teach boys and girls to read, write and do simple arithmetic, and undertake religious study, so one assumes they must have had a fairly good knowledge themselves. Not all of their charges appreciated this teaching. One early, somewhat rebellious, convent girl was Matilda daughter of Henry I and later to briefly become Queen of England in the twelfth century. She was educated at Wilton from the age of thirteen and hated the regulations so much that she tore off her veil in fury, threw it on the ground and trampled all over it.

By 1200 all the major religious orders had orders for women. In England there were twenty-eight female Cistercian houses, twenty-six Benedictine, nine Augustinian and several houses belonging to smaller orders. But this Golden Age of relative equality for nuns within their chosen profession was shortly to disappear.

Between the thirteenth century and the time of the Reformation in the mid-sixteenth century the established thinking of the Church hierarchy began to shift. They were increasingly under pressure to justify their faith in the light of the challenge from the new Protestant thinkers. Hardly surprisingly, women, and religious women in particular, began to be seen as the weak link in the chain. Religious and power conflicts between Pope and Emperor (or Pope and King) typify this period and as a result the Church felt that strength lay in the centralisation of its activities with the power being handed down in a strict descending order of males from God, via the Pope to male members of the religion. The feeling was that their claims to power were threatened if the Church was 'contaminated' by females. Even in the guise of a nun, a woman's body might lead a religious man to temptation. In 1293 Pope Boniface VIII decreed that 'all nuns, present and future, to whatever order they belong shall henceforth remain perpetually enclosed'. What had started out as a spiritual choice to be cloistered in order to pray more devoutly became a virtual prison sentence.

Gradually, under subsequent popes, a nun's privileges were eroded. Her religious life was more closely guarded, being allowed neither to leave the convent nor to have contact with people from the outside world. She was no longer allowed to teach boys and 'dual houses' were phased out. No new female orders could be founded.

It was around this time that a wonderfully shocking and bloody tale emerged; the tale of Pope Joan, the first and, to date, only woman Pope. A young French girl, Joan, disguised as a boy joins the Dominican order. Bright and devout, she rises quickly through the order and is soon called up to Rome and elected Pope. In Rome she fraternises with a young man and on the day of her installation, she gives birth during the procession in the streets and dies a nasty death in the gutters like a common prostitute.

It was a story that became embellished in the telling and was passed on from generation to generation. It also encapsulated all the fears about women's deceitfulness, sexual weakness, frailty and, finally, unfitness to take a role of religious authority. It had a strong element of 'no better than she deserved', a condemnation that was applied to any woman who side-stepped her conventional role. No one at this time chose to remember the attainments of the great Abbesses of Europe.

Despite the change in the Church's party line, women continued to want a religious life. The prevailing climate had become one of chastity and piety, rather than reaching God through religious study. Nuns (and monks to some degree) were losing their access to learning. In the reorganisation, the centres of study passed from monasteries to cathedral chapters (which would evolve into universities like Oxford and Paris). Learning was jealously guarded and there was limited access to these centres. To study one must be ordained and to be ordained one must be a man.

Joining a convent, however, was still a legitimate escape from 'the horrors of childbirth' as Thomas Aquinas put it, and a convent could still offer a rich and full life – albeit in a confined place. Nuns continued to be drawn from noble or propertied families, although working-class girls could join as lay-workers to cook and work the land. Some women joined for personal, spiritual reasons, others arrived sick or in need of refuge. Some girls were sent there by their parents as a way of ensuring their own salvation or simply to get an unmarried daughter into a 'safe place'. Not all the members of a community would be virgins. It was common for widows and older women to take up residence in the convent they had supported whilst they were young.

The days of a medieval nun should, according to the Rule, have passed in silent walking, meditation and prayer, from sunrise to nightfall. In fact, they would have all bent the rules to some degree, making music, singing and writing plainsong. They would have had libraries too; although it was not the classical texts of former years they could spend hours reading and studying if they so wished. Far from quashing creativity, the enclosed rule encouraged artistry, calligraphy, painting frescoes, illumination of manuscripts carried out in a scriptorium, and amazingly ambitious projects such as the Bayeux Tapestry, worked in woollen thread on linen by the nuns.

In the enclosure of nuns the Church hierarchy had overlooked one major consideration. Now that the nuns were forbidden to collect alms outside the convent, or to take in fee-paying pupils, how were they to manage for money? Even with the generous gifts of their benefactresses they could not afford to have their physical needs taken care of by an army of servants whilst they got down to the serious business of praying, as their male superiors would have liked. So, in reality, they took in boarders, sold their produce and crafts and, although unable to teach boys, continued to accept girl pupils. St Michael's Benedictine house, Stamford, was small but typical of the time in this part of England. There were twelve nuns and eight pupils. The richer nunneries of the south might have had thirty to thirty-five nuns and consequently needed to take less pupils.

*

The effect of Henry VIII's anti-catholic 'crusade' and the turbulent years of the Protestant Reformation cannot be underestimated. The sixteenth century was a troubled, frightening and often violent period for Catholics in England and convents took the full force of the King's fury. When in 1533 Henry VIII decided to defy the Pope and divorce Katherine of Aragon, his wife of twenty years, to marry Anne Boleyn it was the signal for decades of upheaval. Church lands and wealth were acquired for the Crown, buildings were demolished; monasteries and convents were 'dissolved'. Catholics, male and female, were persecuted and pursued; many were killed and many were forced to lie low, unable to profess their faith. Amidst this chaos, there was a glimmer of hope for religious women. As in any crisis, it made sense to pull together. Rome relaxed many of the restrictive rules and women in the rest of Europe were once again allowed to start new orders, to teach and care for the sick and poor outside the convent walls.

One of the new orders was the Ursulines, founded by Angela Merici in Italy in the 1530s. She aimed to bring women together to serve God and teach in the Christian spirit. They differed from earlier orders in that they wore no habit, only a simple black or brown dress and they did not remain cloistered. They saw their mission as a battle for the souls of young girls and were advised to get to know each little girl in their charge and protect her from 'the trickery of worldly people'. Again the Church rescinded and the Council of Trent in 1545 made the Ursulines follow the Augustinian rule of wearing a habit and remaining cloistered. It was agreed, however, that their teaching was too valuable for the Church to lose. They were allowed to continue although the pupils now had to come and live with them and study behind closed doors. The Ursulines grew to be the principal way of educating young Catholic girls and a basis for future teaching orders.

In France the convent movement continued to flourish in the seventeenth century with the founding of many new orders, established mostly with the intention of breaking the traditional rules. The most successful of these was the Sisters of Charity which started life as small groups of noblewomen living together in private homes, wearing simple grey dresses and white headdresses and administering to the poor. They got round the cloister rule by retaking their vows each year and spent their time caring for the sick, orphans and children in need. By the 1850s they had become a huge force of nursing sisters, with over 100,000 members.

Treating the sick, where the nuns were under the eye of male doctors, was looked upon more favourably than learning for learning's sake. Learned women were viewed with suspicion – as King James I said in 1603, 'To make women learned and foxes tame has the same effect; to make them more cunning.' In England, Catholic families were sending their daughters abroad to be educated, many of whom stayed on to become nuns. Mary Ward was a product of this system, leaving behind the Catholic persecution of England to join the Poor Clares in St Omer, Belgium. She passionately believed that education for girls was timely and cited the Jesuits who were teaching everywhere to spread the Catholic word. Her philosophy was simple: 'There is no such difference between men and women that women may not do great things!'

There is no doubt that Mary Ward was a woman of extraordinary courage and tenacity. She journeyed back and forth to England to gain support for an Order which would educate rich and poor girls in the community. In practical terms this meant a completely revolutionary way of life for religious women. Non-enclosed and free to travel and work wherever they liked (or wherever God sent them), released from the necessity to pray and sing at fixed hours of the day and free again from male government. The Institute of the Blessed Virgin Mary, as the order was to be known, would be more like a learned college – but one devoted to God. She saw Latin as a vital part of a woman's education realising it was also the key to all forms of serious scientific study, to medicine and to university entrance. Her views, and her brazen dashing across Europe founding schools and convents from Liège to Naples, did not meet with Papal approval. She was attacked by her own Church as wishing to rival men, imprisoned in Germany and finally released to return to England in 1639. Under English law it was illegal to set up schools where the Catholic religion was taught, but wealthy parents flouted the law to send their daughters to Mary Ward's schools. The curriculum was centuries ahead of its time, incorporating Latin, science, mathematics, philosophy, modern languages, literature, drama, music and painting, and a form of debating called 'disputation'. All this at a time when the justification for educating girls at all was simply to enable them to keep books, undertake household management and read from the Bible.

For Protestant girls at the time, education was merely a case of good or bad luck. There might be a good free school in the area or you might have an older brother who did not keep the family tutor fully employed all of the time. For Catholic girls, Mary Ward had re-established the concept of learned, devout women, studying not only for their faith but for their personal development.

Twentieth-century convent girls have a common memory of the hundreds of Catholic 'heroines' with whom they were taught to identify. They often know the lives of these historical women in intimate detail, their hopes and dreams, their trials and their deaths. What all these characters shared was, of course, their faith and a burning passion to follow the Catholic way. Many, like Teresa of Avila who was paralysed before her miraculous recovery, suffered physical pain and illness. Bernadette of Lourdes and Thérèse of Lisieux both died of tuberculosis and their suffering was held up to be praiseworthy in itself. The canonising of these women made them models of behaviour for Catholic girls. Unquestionably these women did perform heroic deeds, facing great danger in their travel and their work. But the nuns chose to emphasise just one side of their extraordinary characters – their compliance, obedience and humility.

This is the paradox that Marina Warner describes in her account. The nuns themselves rarely separated their extraordinary rich and unique history as women from that of the Catholic Church. The irony is that whilst living the independent, uncloistered life of teachers and nuns, which their forbears had fought so hard to achieve, it became part of the tradition to teach their pupils only those elements of history that highlighted the virtues of chastity, humility and obedience.

The late eighteenth and nineteenth centuries saw a wave of new orders established – most of them uncloistered. As the industrial revolution swept through Europe, women were joining the workforce in their droves. The new orders were increasingly focused toward 'useful' work. The Sisters of Mercy, for example, founded in 1841, continued the nursing and charitable work begun by the earlier Sisters of Charity. As the steam-roller of industrialisation moved on, the need for carers to work amongst the new urban poor became glaringly obvious. Religious women responded quickly, first to people's immediate physical needs for food, clothing and basic medical care with soup kitchens and lodging houses, but also to their spiritual and educational needs, 'rescuing' prostitutes and starting 'ragged' schools. Many twentieth century teaching orders were founded by women born into these turbulent times.

Each order had its own particular aims, initially laid down by the foundress. It was unusual for any 1950s schoolgirl not to know the detailed life story of her order's foundress. Even girls attending newly built schools with no old buildings for reference would still be aware that the nuns belonged to an order with its own historical tradition. Some orders, like the Marist Sisters, began in France in the troubled years after the French revolution. Taking Mary as their role model, their foundation was non-cloistered with a preference towards working with the poor. The Salesian Sisters, founded later in the nineteenth century, also had a distinct bias towards disadvantaged children. Other orders were more unashamedly academic. The Society of the Holy Child of Jesus was established in the 1860s to provide Catholic girls with a high standard of education, teaching Latin, German, Italian and Classical Studies at a level usually reserved for the better, boys' public schools. St Leonards-Mayfield school is probably the most famous product of this order – arguably the top Catholic private school in Britain – only rivalled by St Mary's, Ascot run by nuns of the older Order, the Institute of the Blessed Virgin Mary.

A girl joining a convent in 1900 would have had similar tales to tell as one joining in the 1950s. The isolation of convent life combined with the authoritarianism of the Catholic Church resulted in a moribund system that failed to keep pace with the times. What had started life as a radical movement of women, began to be experienced as increasingly oppressive by a new generation of girls. It's at this point that the 'girls' themselves take over the story. Much of their conflict with the nuns and with the Church was the result of this attempt to instil old-fashioned Victorian views of life and sex into them. As for the nuns they were genuinely alarmed by glimpses of life over the convent wall and perceived it as their most urgent duty to fight a rear-guard action on behalf of God and Our Lady.

Jackie Bennett

Maeve Binchy

Maeve Binchy is a best-selling author whose novels and short stories are translated into many languages. She is married to writer and broadcaster Gordon Snell and lives just outside Dublin.

'I think that all of us who have been to convent schools, who thought that this was the only kind of education that there was, now realise that nuns are great box office material. People are very entertained by nuns' stories and we all make them much more horrific than they were.'

The time I was at school was in the late 40s and mid-50s in Ireland, and we were a very backward country then. Everybody believed that a woman's place was in the home and that to take a job that a man could have was almost an unpatriotic act. Every night we would see the long queue of men waiting to catch the mail boat, to go to England to work. Women were not really brought up with the idea of wanting to have a career. That is actually one of the things I can't blame the nuns for – I mean, the poor nuns, they get blamed by everybody for everything! The nuns in our school were English nuns who came over from Britain to teach in Ireland, and they really were as enlightened as any I could find – they hoped we would go on to get degrees.

My father would say the whole time that he was not going to leave us any money – not that any of us wanted any, except perhaps five shillings to go to the pictures more often. But he would say: 'There's going to be no money, but you can all have a great education. You can stay on at university until you die if you like ...' He obviously valued education and in those days in Ireland, an education was absolutely dependent on whether you had enough money to pay your university fees. It was so different from Britain. It became much more enlightened later when we did have an assisted education, if not exactly a free education scheme.

I went to the Convent of the Holy Child in Killarney, about a year after they started and there was a particularly nice nun with whom I am still in contact – Mother St Dominic. We were absolutely desperate to know about the nuns' private lives, wondering what they were like before they went into religion, what their real names were. Now that I'm old enough to ask her I'm not even remotely interested!

There did seem to be a lot of rules, looking back on it. Having your hands clean for lunch seemed to be of equal importance as not telling lies or stealing – and that seemed to me to be as important as not murdering anybody, although perhaps it was just our own interpretation of the rules.

There was one nun who used to say that the bell was the Voice of God, which I found startling. It meant that when the bell rang it was God telling you to move on to the next place. Soon we began to believe it and when the awful electric bell rang we used to roar off to the next place we were going quite sharply! There is one incident I actually put into one of my books and people didn't believe it. One of the nuns came into the classroom one day and stared very hard at a statue of Our Lady. We all stared too – thinking she must be having a vision or something. Her face was deeply disapproving and after about three minutes of this terrible silence she said: 'It is a poor girl who cannot keep the water clean in a vase for Our Lady in the month of May.'

I remember that we were all shocked to the core. There were a couple of flowers dying in front of Our Lady's statue and we were all shocked that it was thought something so heinous and terrible to let the flowers wilt!

I remember other things like that but I really think that all of us who have been to convent schools, who thought that this was the only kind of education that there was at the time, now realise that nuns are great box office material. You see people are very entertained by nuns' stories and we all make them much more horrific than they were. I have never met any girl yet who went to a convent school and who didn't have some kind of joke about turning the lavatory seat up so that the nuns would think that a man had been in the cloakrooms! Or those marvellous stories about not wearing patent leather shoes in case boys could see your knickers reflected in them and would go mad with passion. These are myths and stories that go from one school to another; there was nothing like that at our school.

The nuns' reactions to my books have been generous and full of approval. 'Isn't it lovely to see one of our girls doing so well?' Even when I write rotten nuns into books, as I did in *Echoes*. I felt awfully guilty when *Echoes* was made into a film and the horrible nun was played on the screen. I thought, well now, wasn't that being dreadfully ungrateful to the nice nuns I've met? In *Circle of Friends*, the nun called Mother Frances is not based on any nun I knew, but mainly on myself as a teacher, and therefore any character based on yourself has to be absolutely delightful, warm and lovable because that's the way you think you are!

I think in very simple communities, where the nuns may have entered religious life very young and had no contact with the world, they really did feel afraid that the world outside was full of sin and they had to protect their little charges against it. In our school there was definitely a feeling that once you went out into the world all hell would be let loose, that the gloves would be off and that the possibilities of sin – of every kind, but mainly sins of immorality – would actually be waiting around the corner.

I always set my books in the middle of the 1950s because it was a time of such heightened expectation and great charge for me. I thought the world was going to be full of lust, and it was just waiting. The main thing I would have to do was beat it off because that was what the Church was all about, beating it off until the time was right, and the time would be right within Christian marriage but certainly not before that! I think a lot of this came from my own imagination, but some of it must have come from the nuns.

We never thought it unusual that these women who were not themselves married, who presumably had no knowledge of men, seemed to be an authority on what men would like and wouldn't. One of the things that they were very certain about was that anybody who indulged in any 'loose' behaviour, such as French kissing, would turn the man off forever. He would think: if he kissed a girl who behaved in this very untoward way, how could she possibly be right to be his wife and the mother of his children? The impression was if she did it with him, might she not do it with all others who presented themselves!

I think what has to be remembered is that nobody really believes teachers about anything. Teachers say if you work hard you will get through your exams. They say if you develop the habit of reading young then you will always love reading. You believe neither. So if a nun starts telling you that if you cross your legs Our Lady will blush, or if you say some awful word all the saints in Heaven will put their hands over their ears, I think that it is just one more thing that teachers say. They tell you if you're very good and patient you'll be happy, and that is not so. There were an awful lot of the things we were told *not* to do – like tell long, tall rambling tales in my case. Now I tell long rambling stories which are translated into seven languages and sell in millions all over the world, so I'm very, very glad I didn't listen!

One thing nuns have, that other teachers do not, is their wonderful devotion to duty. I know this because I was a teacher for eight years and I remember children would come up and say: 'Miss Binchy, could you look at this essay . . .?' And I would have one eye on my watch or be going off to meet somebody, or the bus for the weekend was just about to leave. I would say, 'Yes, dear, I will talk to you on Monday about it . . .' Whereas with the nuns, their free time was often spent in the big recreation hall, making charts for the walls and illuminating little posters. We were their life and it was that devotion to duty, I think, which made them so memorable. Most people who were in a convent say the nuns were terribly interested in them, too interested at times. You didn't want the nuns to know your failings, and remember them with such incredible recall when your parents came to the school, but they did! They remembered because they didn't have the social temptations; they didn't have to go home and look after children and a husband. School was their way of life.

Mother St Dominic is the most gifted teacher I have ever met in my life and it is because of her that I became a teacher. In the long hot summer of 1959 I was doing my BA degree and I went over to see her; she had left our school in Killarney and was living in St Leonards-on-Sea. I asked her if I could work with her for a month or two while I was studying for my degree, and maybe she could give me a hand at being a teacher. It was then really, at nineteen going on twenty, that I understood what a really great teacher she was. She used to come and sit in my classroom when I was teaching those little girls and she would tell me afterwards all the things that I had done wrong – or the things that I had done right. I suddenly realised what a great psychologist she was. I did a post-graduate teaching diploma from which I learned absolutely nothing. I learned about McDougall and Freud, and about a man who slept in his coffin, and it was all absolutely useless when I tried to teach. But Mother St Dominic's little skills of understanding the children, of keeping them interested made me suddenly realise that was what she had been doing for us all those years ago. It is a great pleasure that she is still with us and sad that she is not teaching any more.

In my school if you were a 'good' girl you were voted by your companions and the nuns to be a Child of Mary. I was made a Child of Mary in my last year and it really was the most marvellous experience because I was very religious then. You had a candle – I was the only one in the whole school – and I carried the candle out to the top of the church and I said a prayer and I was given a beautiful blue ribbon to wear round my neck with a big medal on it. I was

so proud of it – and so big and jolly with my green school
uniform, I wore this in front of me like a prow of a ship all
the time. It was a wonderful honour. Unfortunately I was
proven not worthy of it.

I was a day girl and in order to court popularity with the
boarders I used to post their letters to their boyfriends on my
way home as they weren't allowed to do this through the
school. I didn't have a boyfriend so it made me closer to this
lovely pulsating, steaming lust which I thought was going on!

One day I met Mother St Dominic who always had a
word and a chat for everybody which, ninety-nine times out
of a hundred, I was delighted with. Unfortunately since I
had the boarders' letters to post this was bad news, so I
stuffed them into the top of my tunic, hoping they would
stay there. But one by one they fell out of my tunic, down to
the ground. She picked them up sadly; they were all
addressed to Master Sean O'Connor or Master somebody
else, to boys in Catholic schools around. They were probably letters of such pathetic innocence, but it was the
deception that mattered. She said, 'I don't think you're
really worthy of being a Child of Mary, are you?' And I had
to admit I wasn't.

I wasn't actually taken up and all my buttons cut off, like
they are in the army, but I handed my medal back to her
privately and my eyes were scarlet from weeping when she
announced at assembly the following Monday that Maeve
Binchy was no longer a Child of Mary. I thought that this
was the worst thing that had ever happened to me in my
whole life. It was the greatest humiliation, and I'd let everybody down – God, Our Lady and my family who were

appalled by it. I must say it was a lovely tribute to the innocence of convent life that you could think that losing your
Child of Mary medal would be the worst thing that could
ever happen to you between now and the grave.

I had so wanted to be a saint, but I remembered that a lot
of the saints went through black periods of great sin and
they were redeemed. There was the parable which I never
understood then, and I don't now, about the prodigal son
who went out, did with the devil 'n'all – and when he came
back there were feasts. The poor good fellow at home was
standing there, with a face as long as a week, saying I've
been here the whole time and nobody's making a fuss of
me. So I thought perhaps the way to sainthood did have to
be spattered with a few bad instances like that. It gave me
some hope.

I felt very safe at the convent. I was growing up at a time
when everything lasted. No one's parents ever split up in
those days and the convent was always there. The nuns didn't
change much and we all felt safe in this very singular society.
We all came from the same kinds of home and we all had the
same religion. The Angelus bell rang at home as it did in the
school. Sometimes the nuns used to ask us to say prayers for
an old Holy Child girl who was going through a crisis of
faith. I don't think they do it now, there's probably too many
prayers to say for too many of us. We used to wonder with
such interest what *kind* of crisis of faith was she going
through? We wouldn't know who she was, she would be from
some English school, but probably marrying a Protestant.
I'd say that was the big crisis of faith. Nothing more danger-
ous than that ever would have come into their lives.

In the 50s, because we were middle-class people, and had enough money to pay for school, we collected toys for the poor at Christmas. I don't think it was until I was about sixteen or seventeen that I realised that it was a patronising thing to do. We'd always bring toys for the crib and one girl would play Our Lady and another would be St Joseph with a lovely little china baby and angels. There was one girl who'd play the ox. She was always very annoyed at playing it. Unfortunately I was never considered reliable enough to play anything because one year I played St Joseph and as I couldn't get the beard off, I was screaming and roaring – too unreliable to take part in plays. We'd sing carols, everybody would bring a toy and we'd put it beside the crib and at the end the nuns would give it to the poor with a capital P. We used to give a lot of money to the missionaries in those days too. I used to raise stick insects. If I saw one now I'd have to go into intensive care, they're awful things with legs on them, they used to eat nothing but privet. Absolutely revolting, but for some reason we all had a great interest in them at school, and I used to sell them I think at 3d each in aid of the missions. We gave a lot of money and saw nothing odd in going out to another country and changing its way of life because we thought it was a good thing. If they had no clothes, they must have clothes, and then of course they must have faith. If you had the faith and you went through life and didn't give it to other people, it would be very, very selfish. So we supported the missions like mad.

I didn't realise how interesting it is to other people when you suddenly say you believed absolutely for years and years – and then gave it up. I often get letters from people begging me to go back. It's just that in my heart I don't feel there is anything after this world. I feel that any wrongs have to be righted here. I can't imagine that I'd ever again have the same wonderful clarity that God was an Irishman with a big smile, that the angels all knew me personally, and that St Patrick would be talking about me and saying that I'd be coming up to Heaven soon. All the lovely safety and beautiful technicolor pageants that I had in my childhood. I can't imagine it coming back again but it's my loss really. I envy the people who are able to keep it. I don't feel haunted by it, I don't feel guilty. I feel that if there is a God and I've abandoned him, well, He must be saying, 'There she is, self-ish, stupid person . . .', but I don't think it's coming after me the whole time and I don't feel that in times of crisis or danger I would turn to it.

But you never know, I've known people who have felt exactly the same way as I did and on their deathbed or when they are approaching the end of their life, they change and offer appeasement.

Clare Boylan

Clare Boylan was born and grew up in Dublin where she attended two convent schools. An award-winning journalist, she turned to fiction and now enjoys widespread success for novels such as *Holy Pictures*, *Room for a Single Lady* (winner of the Spirit of Light Award) and *Beloved Stranger* and for her short story collections. She is the editor of non-fiction anthologies such as *The Literary Companion to Cats* and *The Agony and the Ego*, essays on the art of contemporary fiction. Her seventh novel, published in 2003, is *Emma Brown*, a continuation of an 18-page fragment written by Charlotte Bronte before her death.

'We took it so much for granted that we would go to Heaven, the same way that when you grow up you take it for granted you will fall in love. Then you suddenly realise there isn't instant access ...'

My sisters were older than me, the spoilt little brat of the family. While my mother was indulging me at home, they kept saying, 'Wait until you get to school, you will get beaten with a chair leg every day ...' The overriding quality of my life at home was boredom. I was sheltered and protected, I wasn't allowed to do anything so I *knew* school was going to be terribly exciting when I got there.

I went to two different types of convent. I started out in 1954 at a Presentation Convent which gave a very simple education. We were constantly told not to rise above our station in life, but one did learn to spell very well, to read and do mental arithmetic and I think that is not a bad achievement.

It was rather wonderful as a convent girl always to be with adults who knew a little less than you did. We were innocent, we were children, but however poorly equipped we were, the nuns always had a little less information about life. I thought that was tremendous fun. I think also that it gave us children a feeling of solidarity. We did not compete with each other. Generally, I think, convent girls are very loyal to each other and that they make great friends.

For my secondary education I went to the fee-paying, middle-class St Louis Convent where there was a totally different atmosphere. Irony was used in place of corporal punishment, the nuns were less ingenuous and there was a strenuously competitive air with a great emphasis on debating societies and public competition. The nuns were ambitious socially and academically and I think the girls did rather well out of that school. When you meet past pupils they all seem to have good careers. It was always assumed that we would marry, the nuns did assume that, but the girls seemed to make their professional mark as well.

One of the problems with convent schools is that the emphasis really is on a spiritual education and so any literature that connects to the sensual or erotic is immediately off the agenda and this limits one's receptivity to further education. There was no appreciation of art or knowledge for its own sake. The alternative to learning was life. You got out, ran like mad and got on with it. I did not go on to university. When I look back, I think it's a pity, but at seventeen, I would certainly not have been ready for academic development.

We were always told not to answer back and I have never quite figured out what that meant. It meant you weren't meant to look for elaboration on any information offered, I think. I suppose we were reasonably well mannered – if anything a bit subdued, which is probably why we rebelled when we grew up – but I don't think we were particularly more polite than other children.

In Ireland we didn't have nursery stories, it wasn't the tradition, but the saints took their places and as with all nursery stories they had a touch of the macabre. The nuns were particularly fond of child saints like Maria Goretti. Nowadays children all have Winnie the Pooh bears to carry around with them. We had statues of the saints and it was nice because you could actually talk to them in church. They would intercede for you and this was a kind of magic – I mean we saw it in this way. It is a pity we didn't have little statues to take to bed with us. It would have been very comforting, you know.

When we were small we were taught by a nun who ran our school branch of the Pioneers of Total Abstinence Association. This was where, at the age of ten, convent girls gave up their degenerate habits and renounced drink for life! What one did at the meetings was dwell on the sufferings of Christ, on the understanding that every time a glass of alcohol passed your lips you were putting Him through the crucifixion again. This poor woman was a sado-masochist *manqué* and in order to improve our meditations she would describe the crucifixion in the most depraved and gruesome way. She would say, 'Picture the head of Christ with thorns two inches long piercing his skull, imagine the blood gushing forth . . .' We had bondage and we had flagellation. There is no doubt about it, the woman was obsessed, her thoughts were violently disturbed. And all these little kids sat there, goggle-eyed, listening. I can't say it had any lasting effect. We thought it was terribly intcresting.

I think that my upbringing as a Catholic, a Catholic *girl*, has influenced every line I write, although I don't actually write that much about it. My first novel, *Holy Pictures*, had a convent setting, but I was not writing about it as my background. It was more as a universal symbol for aspiration to the unattainable. We took it so much for granted that we would go to Heaven, the same way that when you grow up you take it for granted you will fall in love. Then you suddenly realise there isn't any instant access to Heaven. It makes a very good symbol, a universal symbol for expectation and ambition, that I think anybody with a Jewish background would probably understand.

I have also used specific incidents which I have adapted, as one does for fiction. In *Holy Pictures* there is an episode when the central character gets the great honour of being chosen to play the fairy in the school concert. In fact she is the nuns' pet but she's rather too big for the fairy because she's got a bust, which is a bit of a disgrace. Also, she has come under the influence of the cinema, she's been watching the stars and how they move – that languorous way women move for the purpose of sexual attraction. She is a bit bored with the whole thing so she decides to develop her little dance and all the men in the audience are absolutely transfixed. There is a frightful scandal afterwards because she does this dance which bears more resemblance to the dance of the seven veils than her fairy dance.

When I was fourteen we were entered for a drama competition by a very ambitious nun. She wrote the play (in Irish), cast it, directed, hired costumes, but then being a nun, she wouldn't actually come along to the finals, which were staged in a theatre in the city. We had to pick up our own costumes on the way to the theatre, including the wonderful full-length bridal gown which I was to wear in my starring role.

We collected the hamper and arrived at the theatre with just time to get dressed, but something had gone wrong with the costumes and instead of my wedding dress there was a sort of ballet tutu, but it was quite a sexy little thing. It was a chorus girl's outfit, or something similar. We didn't know what to do, but we were due on stage and there was no adult to advise us. So we pinned on various layers of tulle from other costumes and the effect got more and more absurd. All the other finalists were from boys' schools so the theatre was full of these very spotty little boys. I had to stand on stage for an hour or more while the action unfolded around me and the boys gaped, enchanted. At that time – 1964 – the catch cry among rude little Dublin boys was, 'Get them off yer!' They followed girls, shouting, 'Get them off yer!' so throughout the play the Damer Hall rang with cries of 'Get them off yer!' We won Best Play, Best Direction and even Best Actress, but nobody was terribly pleased with us and it ended my dramatic career.

Although I don't recall much of my catechism I do remember scruples. There were actually books of scruples with questions like: If you were in an accident and were knocked unconscious and someone forced a cup of tea between your lips and you didn't know, would you commit a mortal sin by going to communion without having fasted? We did worry about things like that, questions regarding fasting in particular. If one drank a glass of water, had one broken the fast? What if the water was *warm*?

I loved Benediction. I still love joss sticks, the closest evocation of that theatrical swinging of the thurible with its clouds of scented smoke. I loved the feast of Corpus Christi when we dressed up in our old Communion dresses for the procession. We wouldn't let them go, we went on wearing them for years and years, with slips hanging down underneath and busts growing. We walked through the streets, singing hymns and scattering flowers, with huge banners carried overhead. Afterwards, we always ate a bag of chips on the way home. I quite miss all that. Corpus Christi is an aggressively sensual idea, if you think about it, because the whole of the Catholic faith is based on mysticism, on the idea that our bodies are irrelevant, that we are destined for the immortal life of the spirit – and yet this is the celebration of the body of Christ (as of course is the Eucharist) and not the spirit.

I do think all the emphasis on the mortification of the flesh put an enormous concentration on our bodies. We might not have thought about them that much but we were permanently brought back to the flesh, its weakness, its temptations, its appetites. While it was understood that all men were after the one thing, it was always a woman's business to stop them. Men had no control. It was entirely a woman's fault!

Katie Boyle

Katie Boyle was born Caterina (Irene Elena Marie) Imperiali di Francavilla, the daughter of an Italian marquis. Her parents divorced when she was very young and she was brought up by her father and his second wife, a woman thirty years his senior. She was educated at several schools in Italy but her lasting and happy memories are of the Sacred Heart Convent in Rome. Her autobiography *What This Katie Did* written in 1980 told the story of her turbulent childhood. She now lives in north London with her three previously stray dogs. She calls them her 'liquorice allsorts' as they consist of one white poodle, one collie-cross and a tiny Italian greyhound.

'When I go into a rough area and think the going might be heavy, I still put out my hand and ask my guardian angel to look after me.'

I attended six schools and was expelled from four of them. My parents were told that the school could get on very well without me which I think was the expression that was used at the time. The one I really loved and have a great deal of affection, respect and a lasting love for was the Sacred Heart in Rome.

I loved that place; the nuns were so understanding, so broadminded, so worldly and yet not at all worldly. I think I got my values from them. I had a wonderful stepmother, but apart from her I think I owe a tremendous amount to the nuns – I was very happy there. The nuns were extremely intelligent and well educated themselves, they came from backgrounds that had understanding in them and they did not try and hold the reins all the time. There was a wonderful thing that Mother Superior used to do: she had a little notebook that she gave to all the children. In this notebook we were allowed to pour out our hearts. I don't know how she managed to read them all, my writing was totally illegible, even at that age. At the end she just put one comment or if you were lucky you got three lines. It was wonderful; it was also something instructive, it was always something that made you think. So you didn't ever feel alone, you felt that somebody really cared about you, about what you felt and how you were reasoning.

I think it had discipline and, rather like I believe in having well-trained children and well-trained dogs, I think that a happy child is a child who does have fair discipline. They scored again on this count. You feel that you are important, that you're being given your head, that you're being allowed to develop. Their teaching was very good, they didn't try and cram you with information. They taught you how to learn and even now this is very important to me; if I don't know something you can bet your boots I know how to find it out – that's why I was a good agony aunt.

There was always laughter; there was discipline, of course, but there was always fairness. My husband goes mad because I can't really write an article or really concentrate unless there is noise around me. I can have the television and the radio on because at the Sacred Heart we were made to do our homework in an enormous hall where there was always something going on. The doors were open, people went to and fro, somebody would come to talk to the Mother who was in charge and none of us ever lifted our heads; we got on with it, and this was something I appreciated and which has had long lasting effects.

There was also a great deal of encouragement. We had awards like the Ruban Rouge and the Ruban Blue – the Red Ribbon and the Blue Ribbon – and they were what you aimed for. It wasn't because you were goody-goody but because you had a sense of initiative, or that you were good with other children and that you were a good mixer. After all a school is a microcosm of what is coming next and I think it taught us how to behave out in the wide world.

The Sacred Heart has branches all over the world and

when I came to England I could make contact here with the Sacred Heart. We were speaking in the same language immediately. Mary was our role model. In the painting she was still studying in the temple, so she wasn't already the Mother of Jesus and therefore we could identify with her as a child. This is something that I have always had, this great devotion to the Madonna because I know she saw me through school, so she will see me through the rest.

I do recollect that we did keep our shirts on when we had a bath and I also recollect that I took mine off as soon as I was in the water. I don't think that anybody said anything terrible to me. I think that they were of a generation that were beginning to shed the shirt as we might say. I remember my beloved Mother Sunger. When they caught me for *This Is Your Life* they brought her over from Germany. The first thing I saw when she turned up on the programme was her legs. I said: 'Your legs!' and she looked at me and said: 'Caterina you are so old-fashioned!' I think that sort of modesty has changed.

People don't believe it but in Rome it can be very cold and we didn't have running water; we had basins and jugs to wash with. I remember very often breaking a layer of ice on the water. It was so cold, it's amazing I haven't got a lot of broken veins because that's one of the ways to get them, to wash your face in ice cold water. But the other thing I always remember was the real agony of having to get up at dawn and go to Mass on an empty stomach. Apart from the embarrassment of holding it in so that it didn't gurgle, it was the actual feeling of nausea that one had. The other occupational hazard of going to a convent is of course scraped knees, knees that get hardened by kneeling. When you came to spend your holidays *not* going to Mass every day you spent your time putting cream on them to make them soft again. Even at that early age I was quite vain. I didn't want to have knees that showed I'd gone to Mass and spent so much time kneeling. I used to put a lot of cold cream on my knees and used lots of hot water.

The church itself was a public church which was divided by wrought iron gates so that the public was behind the gates and the girls of the convent were in front nearer the altar. The great thing was you used to see the big wide world through those gates but you only had one moment to look and that was as you first came into the church. We used to slow right down, at least I used to, and scan everybody to see if anybody I knew was there. You looked and you hoped that somebody might come. I had a boyfriend who I was so mad about at the very tender age of fourteen. He used to come whenever he could escape and he always came to see me at Mass so I slowed down to a snail's pace. Mother Garnier would say: 'Come along, hurry up to your places!'

The outside world was very much outside when we were there. The convent was right at the top of the Spanish Steps – one of the classic tourist views of Rome. It was an oasis of peace up there looking over the Piazza di Spagna. We would walk up the side steps to a big wooden door with its wrought iron nails and when that shut behind you, you were suddenly in the cloisters. I thought it was lovely; you couldn't even hear the traffic. I found it very reassuring, after all those other schools, I thought I belonged. I loved it.

I didn't want to get out. I think I appreciated this womb-like quality probably because I had such a fiery time at home.

They basically taught us right from wrong. It was in the 1940s and in those days you didn't have to tell children that there were certain things one did or did not do. A chaste kiss was going a long way. I know when my boyfriend threw roses across the wall and a rose was found by a nun and brought in, it wasn't really done with any great sense of: Oh you have been very wicked. It was more a case of: It isn't time yet; there is a time for everything. They wanted us to know that there was a big wide world out there, which we would become a part of in good time.

There was one class which I really liked called 'Bearing/Deportment'. It taught me how to walk into a room, how to sit down, how to cross my legs; and they used to say: 'We don't cross our legs but you will have to, so we will teach you how to do it gracefully.' They taught us how to walk into a room and how not to slink in like a little mouse. You walk in and you're proud to be a woman and this has the most tremendous effect. I can kid anybody that I have all the confidence in the world when my knees are trembling and I'm on the verge of tears. They instilled in us the pride of being a woman, proud of being somebody who expected respect.

They gave us self-esteem. There is a very fine line between self-esteem and conceit. Conceit was not encouraged. On the contrary it was slapped down. If you thought you were something you weren't, or if you thought you could do something better than somebody else you were told that humility is one of the most important qualities that a girl can have. Don't ever get swollen-headed.

I think we were happy. I think the idea of not teaching religion in schools is where children of future generations are going to lose out. It is no good saying, as a parent, I will let my child choose for himself when he or she gets older, because unless you have something to begin with, certain rules and regulations, there's nothing to go by. I don't mind what religion, but you must be taught the right and wrong in life then you will be in a position to choose what you want to do whether you want to become a Buddhist or whatever. I don't think that this lax attitude is going to benefit children in any long-term way. I think the rules that are learnt at school through religion are of vital importance to you as a person.

I remember very clearly the sensory aspects of the convent. The incense in the church, the indefinable smell, the 'whooshing' of the nuns' clothes, and they all wore long clothes. I'm sure it's much more comfortable for them now, but there was a lovely cleanliness about them, there was a lovely soap smell, not scented soap; it was very reassuring. I feel that this was what gave one strength in later life; to know that there is such a place; such peace, such strength, such charm, that there is such rectitude. I loved that. I loved rushing along the corridors and then suddenly seeing the Mother Superior and doing a curtsy on the run. I was an expert at that, and I never tripped once. I must say it wasn't much of a curtsy, it was more of a bob.

I have often bargained with the Madonna saying: 'Now, look, if I am a good girl and I really do this, I will swap if you will do that for me.' I know one serious one was when my stepmother was told she had cancer and that she had to have her breast removed. I said: 'Look, if I don't touch butter for the whole of this term, even if it is in cooking   I will pretend that it is not there ... will you please get her well and will you let her be well all the summer when I am there.' Well, she probably would have been anyway but she certainly was at her most healthy that summer. She died five or six years later but I felt that I had pleaded and done something for Jesus. We are great believers that the souls in purgatory will benefit from our offerings. We were always offering something up to the souls in purgatory. If I fell down I used to say I am not going to cry because if I don't it will help a soul in purgatory. I had no illusions at all that they'd get out earlier and then I'd be helped when I got over there. It was a good sort of bargaining practice.

I am a great believer that there's total continuity between one world and the next and I think if we can keep this feeling it's extremely helpful. I still go across the road and if I think it's going to be nasty I surreptitiously put my hand out to the right and say to my guardian angel: 'Help me across will you?' I am not ashamed of it. I don't know why I do it surreptitiously. I suppose it would be rather funny if I put out my hand to nobody. I've had a very full life, I'm still having a very full life. If I have had any success at all it is in relationships: I think that the convent education has helped enormously with friendships, with the values that I have, with my marriage – my marriages ... I hate to say it because this is really a contradiction in terms because as a convent girl I shouldn't have had three marriages. I had a very friendly divorce to begin with, then I was widowed after twenty-three years and now I've been married for eleven years.

My father divorced my mother when I was very young and then he married a sweet woman who was sixty years old when he was a mere thirty. She was a remarkable woman because she took on a child of five, a very lively child and put a stamp on her. She had a tremendous effect on me. It was a combination of my stepmother and the Convent of the Sacred Heart that have helped me through my later life. I hate children who say terrible things about their parents, but my father wasn't an easy person. He was a megalomaniac, a schizoid and that's all I'm prepared to say. He certainly made a hash of a lot of people's lives. I do think that my religion did help me then. He put me into these schools and therefore I cannot say anything too terrible about him because he obviously wanted to give me a good basis for my life. I'm torn; I'm torn by my feelings of hate as well as love for him but I will always have to acknowledge that he gave me strength by choosing the Sacred Heart Convent.

Carmen Callil

Carmen Callil was born in 1938 in Melbourne, Australia to a mother of Irish Catholic, and a father of Catholic Lebanese descent. Her father was a barrister and lecturer in French at Melbourne University and died when Carmen was nine years old. She was sent to convent boarding schools from the age of four. The first, Star of the Sea Convent, Gardenvale was run by Presentation nuns and was the same school that Germaine Greer attended as a senior. Carmen stayed there only until she was nine and was then transferred to Mandeville Hall convent run by Loreto nuns. She read English and History at Melbourne University and on the day she graduated took the boat out of Australia for good.

Carmen spent the 60s in 'swinging London' working as an editorial assistant and a publicist. She started Virago Press in 1972 'to publish books which were a product of the new women's movement', at first in tandem with Quartet. Four years later, in September 1976, an independent Virago Press was launched. She remained Chair of Virago until 1995 and was also Managing Director and Publisher of Chatto and Windus from 1982 until 1993. She is now a critic and writer, currently working on a book about Vichy France.

'There are good things about the Catholic Church that I see through a very smoky glass, but the bad thing about it, particularly with regard to women, is its investment in suffering.'

My first convent was attached to the local parish church, St James's, Gardenvale and it was a large grey building with a big asphalt playground and high walls. The second was in a beautiful building called Mandeville Hall. It was a very beautiful Victorian building set in grassy gardens. I have nightmares about both buildings. I could tell you every single room. I drove to Mandeville Hall once to have a look. I got to the gate and turned around. I couldn't face it, or I could face it but I didn't want to.

I dream about this path going up to the grand front door and I'm in this terrible queue, this crocodile, and I'm permanently stuck there, trapped in this nightmare place, mindlessly marching somewhere.

They are terrible memories. The place had cold grey walls and there was tremendous physical discomfort. People think Australia is enormously hot, but in fact Melbourne has very cold winters. There was never any central heating in our day, and so everybody got very bad chilblains. My best friend from school actually still has hands that are completely scarred by the chilblains. It was such a class-ridden place and I always remember the poor Irish nuns, the little Irish girls who were Sisters, never Mothers. Their hands used to bleed and their chilblains used to bleed as they scrubbed and did the dishes. It was horrible.

The greatest ambition of the nuns of the Institute of the Blessed Virgin Mary was that one should be a lady. They were not interested in academe at all. They certainly were not interested in you doing anything afterwards except becoming a good Catholic mother. It was a tremendous battle. I was always trying to be a good Catholic you see, that's the point. I thought that was what God wanted, so I always tried terribly hard. I was incredibly conventional. I was quite good at sport, but I was very good at my lessons. I always came top of the class. I loved my lessons and I tried to be a good student and do things properly, but it was no good. Those nuns weren't interested in having children who might fulfil themselves in different ways, or grow up to be happy. They were interested in having children who would be driven into some sort of Catholic mould that would then continue, with more Catholics of exactly the same kind. Obedience, really. They were interested in you obeying what you were told; you were not meant to think.

I remember once I was weeping over some absolute catastrophe – I can't recall what the catastrophe was, but I was walking down the green verandah outside the classrooms, weeping. This nun who taught music, whom I was also quite fond of, rushed up to me and said: 'Offer it up for the Poles! Offer it up for the Poles!' I don't know what was happening to the Poles at that time, but she certainly wasn't interested in what was happening to me.

Our sex education was short and simple. We had a meeting in the school hall, and this priest came in and he drew a lot of organs on the blackboard. Sideways as well, which is a very peculiar way to look at them. And that was it. We very rarely saw a priest, so you realised that this was something major, that a male had entered the establishment. Priests came to say Mass and then they went.

I was a quiet, terrified little girl really and I think the nuns were quite suspicious of me. I was traumatised by that convent – I'd say it took me about fifteen years to get over it. For example, I got scruples; I wouldn't speak, which is a sort of anorexia. I'd say to myself: It will be a mortal sin if I speak. I was always taking what they said to me to its logical conclusion and they were constantly telling me how you commit mortal sins. I just couldn't deal with it. It was ghastly – I actually left the country to get away from that.

I never talk to other Catholics or to anybody about the convent because it was such a bad time in my life. I've obliterated it. I've only started thinking about it again for this [TV] programme. When you're a child you don't understand why you've done wrong. You're always doing wrong in an unexplained way, because reason isn't on the agenda. The guilt is still there. I sort of put up with it and I say: Carmen, not again. But everything I do is despite myself because of that guilt. You're guilty about everything.

I think the nuns actually had a vested interest in suffering. The Catholic Church represents various things. There are good things about it that I see through a very smoky glass, but the bad thing about it, particularly with regard to women, is its investment in suffering. They had a rather perverted enjoyment of narrowing little children down, squashing them and making them suffer. But you see these nuns are programmed women. They're programmed to exclude everything that doesn't follow the narrow little path they've chosen as the path of life.

This is the only part of my life that I think upon with dismay. I mean you've chosen to interview me about something I will never forgive, or can't forgive, because it scarred me so much. Everything else that happened to me in my life pales into insignificance in comparison with what those nuns did to me. Thank God you have parents and brothers and sisters and friends and you have your brain. I think you have God as well. I don't think God approves of these people – I think he was on my side. God and I continue to negotiate life. I think I am still a Catholic. I talk to God, I just don't talk to them.

Michael Holroyd gave me *Frost in May* to read, and I read it over a weekend. I was absolutely suffused with misery and agony and fury as I read it because I identified with it so much. It told what I felt to be my own story. Not that it *was* my own story, but the suffering it conveyed and the feeling of mindless repression which the child couldn't deal with because the child didn't understand what was going on and what the reasons were. I felt so strongly about it that I actually invented Virago Modern Classics to enable me to publish that book. The world had to read the book again. It told everyone what it was like to be traumatised by nuns and have your life more or less ruined by them.

Of the girls I went to school with I've got two friends left. I hardly ever see the others. But of the two who are still friends I think their view of the convent would be less hostile than mine, and less violent. Neither of them are practising Catholics; the only friends I've got left are ones who gave it all up too.

Every time I go home to Australia they say, come on, it's changed so much since your day. Maybe so, but they should pay for what they did to those children. That section of my life is scarred forever, but I've made up for it in other ways!

Polly Devlin

Born in 1944, Polly Devlin is a well-known broadcaster and writer. Her books include *The Far Side of the Laugh*; a novel, *Dora*; a book of essays, *Only Sometimes Looking Sideways* and her first book *All of Us There* was re-published as a Modern Classic by Virago in 2003. She has received an OBE for services to literature.

'I know a lot of girls who were at my convent school who really didn't ever raise their heads above the parapet and who I think were so damaged that there's no repairing the damage. Those silent people, with their voices locked into their throats, I think, suffered a lot.'

I was a terrifically anxious child. Anxious to please, anxious to do good, anxious that the world might end. Anxiety was a kind of water-mark that underlaid every day of my life. When I look back on it now, from this perspective, I think what was that all about? My parents were so secure, there was so much there and yet … it was as if I was living in a marsh or boggy place. At any moment I might fall down into it. I'm not sure what did that. Whether it was the whole genetic thing of being Irish, which sounds far-fetched – unless you're Irish in which case it isn't or whether even, at a very early stage it was to do with being a Catholic. It's paradoxical; your Faith was supposed to be built on a rock, yet far from being a rock, the Irish Catholic faith was a most extraordinary quicksand. So, perhaps from a very early age the Catholic Church played a part in my anxiety. Equally it might be in my genes that I'm anxious, but certainly school made me more anxious.

The first convent school I went to was the more liberal. They were Belgian nuns and rather grand. I was much happier there, given that I was not a happy child, but the authority the nuns had was absolutely terrifying. I think it's gone, that sense of authority being so much in command that those in your charge could *die* on command.

In the primary school I liked the teachers and they were

kind, but it was a system of absolute rigidity. If a child left her desk, anarchy would result, so even to get out of the classroom to go to the lavatory was quite an act of rebellion, just to put up your hand and ask to go. The teachers there, native Irish, always used very harsh words. The teacher would say that she would *massacre* you or people would say, 'I'll *kill* you for that,' when in fact they meant 'I will speak quite strictly to you.' One was always in a sense living on a knife-edge of violence, which did not occur.

I don't know what they were so afraid of. I think it was a leftover from Victorian times, and earlier, when children were seen but not heard. There are specific moments impressed on my mind when the general atmosphere of anxiety was magnified into fear, when the black-robed priest came in and asked us questions about religion. So much hung in the balance. You could see that not only was the teacher anxious that we should answer well, but that the fate of the school hung on whether or not you answered the question. Nor did you answer the questions about Catholicism and faith from any kind of feeling of belief or knowledge. You answered it according to rote, according to how you'd learned it out of your little cate-chism. You chanted it like a mantra, these long convoluted answers to: What is the Eucharist? What does Baptism mean? What does the state of Grace mean? You answered it exactly according to rote, and if you dropped a word or put in a word, it was the wrong answer. It was astonish-ingly authoritarian, nothing whatsoever to do with intellectual curiosity, or freedom, or tolerance – God forbid!

I can still remember a lot of the answers because I occasionally bring them up in my writing, and they seem to be hinges of a kind. Not hand-holds or atavistic lifebelts, but a kind of parallel mad philosophy. In *Dora*, a novel I've written, there's a violent moment when Dora is taking a shower and something happens to her, and she says by rote the answer to, What is Baptism? That comes singing up – or crying up – within her, and that's based directly on my experience; not the violent moment, but the resurrection of the effort towards absolute certainties.

It seems to me that humiliation and humility were far too close together to be healthy. The virtues of humility and modesty seem to me to be great qualities and yet 'humility' in the convent sense seemed to be missing something. If I were humble, if I had humility I wouldn't write – because silence is a form of humility and one I admire very much in the disciplines of closed orders, for example, and in people who do, literally, keep their mouth shut. On the other hand, if you listen to a lark singing, or you hear Wordsworth when he's in full throat, you understand that silence is not necessarily one of the great qualities. Humility was so much mixed up with a lack of self-esteem in our dispensation that it turned into humiliation. In our system if you allowed your natural exuberance and natural energy (and I have a lot of energy) to emerge it was viewed as pride, or vanity or as an unacceptable grab for attention. And so you became a notice box, or you became *bold*: 'You're a bold girl.' Bold in the English language is a marvellous word. It's swashbuckling, energetic. It's going where someone else hasn't gone. But bold in that Irish usage meant bad, aggressive, forward. You wanted to get yourself looked at. But why *not* get yourself looked at? What was so inherently wrong in drawing attention to yourself? It goes back to the idea of modesty, and of course to the distorted image of men we were presented with, men as rampant lunatics who at the least encouragement were going to fall on you and turn you into Maria Goretti. It was a most horrible system because humility, which was a virtue, was denigrated into humiliation. The more abashed you could become the more agreeable you were in the sight of God. That's not a good way to rear children, it's not a legacy that I would want my children to have at all, where self-effacement became self-abasement.

In the end it was self-defeating because you became so determined not to be put down by it, that you manufactured more energy and became more competitive in order to assert yourself. I don't know whether one is born a writer, but certainly I think writers are egocentric and ego-maniacal and my expressions in print are to do with saying, 'Look at me, this is not sinful, I won't be put down.'

The obverse side of this is that I know a lot of girls who were at my convent school who were almost literally put down, who really didn't ever raise their heads above the parapet and who I think were so damaged that there's no repairing the damage. Those silent people, with their voices locked into their throats, I think, suffered a lot.

It was so easy to have warped ideas about sex from your education that I can't think how you would have come out with different ones. Sensuality was not just a sin, it was unspeakable. It was the primrose path. It was tied up with

this 'being a notice box' – any 'flowering' wasn't held to be
a good thing.

The second school I went to has changed considerably
now but in the time I was there it was very damaging. The
way the nuns dressed decried and denied all sex, all belief
that they were womanly. They wore their hair (which is such
an important expression of one's sensuality) covered up with
a wimple, so the face became blinkered. There was something so sexless about that face. People talk about the
serenity and the purity and the feeling of peace that came
out of it. I never did find that serenity. I just found those
hooded black things like vultures, about to pounce on me.
The swish of their huge wide-bodied skirts as they came
round the corner still gives me a chill when I think of it.
They had a scapula that fell from this white, chaste thing
that covered bosom and breast, so that what you saw was a
black bird-like figure, completely sexless, coming at you –
and these were our mentors. Girls who were budding into
adolescence and into womanhood were being taught by
these extraordinarily mediaeval figures, jumped out of some
extraordinary Gothic painting, telling them how to live.
These were women who had eschewed all spirit, all sensuality, turned their backs on earthly delights, had taken a
vow of chastity and who, in every possible predication you
can think of, were held up to us as being better than our
own mothers, as having made the greater choice, the Marys,
rather than the Marthas.

I think that the greatest thing is to have and rear children
and to know another human being in the fullness of love
including sex. Yet I think back to myself going to confession

to a celibate priest who believed – who *had* to believe – that sex was wrong. I had to tell him what sins I'd committed. And the nuns did not believe that any form of sex could be right. Sex and sensuality was something to be struggled against and to be overcome. Again – it's not something I would want my own children to have to learn.

I think on the whole that the Irish are not a visual race. Their talent for expression lies not in painting or in decoration but in words and that's easily enough traced to a history that allows you to carry nothing in your hands. You carry it in your head and you carry it in your language. Oral expression is extremely important if you haven't got great libraries and great art galleries. We had no pictures to look at, but we were brought up on a kind of 'religious pornography', the paintings and representations in every church, all of which were extraordinarily gory and gruesome. There were the details of the Stations of the Cross and pictures of bleeding hearts, literally, torture: Maria Goretti being chopped up, St Lucy with her breasts cut off – saints being broken on the wheel. There was terrific emphasis placed on suffering. There's one famous and much loved Irish hymn, 'Faith of Our Fathers', in which one pleads that our children may be tortured to death for the faith. You get a sense of hotting the congregation up from seeing these extraordinarily gory images, from singing such hymns and I think it's downright unhealthy.

I have no happy memories of convent life and so it is a very anxious time, talking to you like this, because what you're talking to is not a grown-up woman at ease in her environment. I'm kicked back into what I was when I talk about nuns – a child who was desperately anxious to please, who never got praised because praise was something that might make you prideful. So no matter what you did it was never enough.

Even when they got you dressed up to go on your May Day procession you never knew when you were going to arbitrarily be called up and told that you had been sucking your teeth, or looking out of the window, or that you hadn't been saying your prayers. You had done *something* that you were going to be screamed at or scolded for. It isn't just my imagination, I think I had a natural energy and I wanted to be loved and looked at. That desire attracted attention and so it had to be 'beaten out of me' – for my own good, you understand.

One of the more poignant and memorable moments – like a Dickensian scene – is of being beaten fiercely over my hands because I coughed in chapel. I coughed like a walrus every time I went into the chapel; I didn't cough the rest of the time. Of course the cough was induced – it was my only way of getting attention. And of course it was maddening, but you don't have happy memories if somebody has swiped you ten times because you've coughed. You think: how *could* they do that to a sick child? If you were the nun you thought differently, you thought: that child is coughing on purpose and I'm going to beat it out of her.

The statistics on the number of Irish men suffering from schizophrenia are quite horrifying. What is odd is that it's not just in Ireland, it's in the enclosed emigrant communities in Canada as well. But think of a system where a man is brought up to believe that women are so pure they can never be sullied, where women are brought up to believe they can never be sullied (and even the word 'sullied' is already a denigratory term), where any expression of sex is inherently wrong. Since a young man's or woman's system is geared to reproduction and to sex, that system will naturally start to go sad under such a regime. What should be an expression of joy becomes an expression of evil, and it must turn in on itself; it seems obvious that if a whole part of yourself that is so important – the urge to reproduce, the urge towards sex, the celebratory will to live – is presented as evil, dark, dank, something that takes place in closed rooms, something that you confess afterwards; if it's presented that way then something that should be such a joyful flowering is driven in on itself. It must put devastating pressure on the mind, I think, in a way almost like mushrooms – I once read of a trapdoor, an enormous slab of a trapdoor which, over 400 years, was pushed up by the growth of mushrooms – the extraordinary slow strength just pushing it up. I think that sex is like that, not over 400 years, over quite a short time. You repress it, it comes up in another rather more poisonous growth and that poisonous growth I think knocked a lot of people's minds out of kilter.

Yet for all that I'm so vehement and so passionate about it I don't suffer many long-term effects. I began to work out that it was so ludicrous that I must distance myself from it and in a sense I was given something very valuable by that education, if only a celebratory sense of life. When something has been taken away from you or is held slightly out of reach, you look at it very longingly, you want it so much. When you attain it, either it isn't worth the candle, or else it's so precious that you handle it with *great* care. I think (I hope) I got to the point where I accepted what happened to me was part of the whole of my life. Then the lack of humiliation, the lack of humility, the lack of fear of sensuality, the lack of fear of sex became absolute celebrations in themselves.

One of the memories that has had a real effect on my life is the absolute cleanliness and calmness and positioning of things in the convent. The floor shone. There was a wonderful smell of polish. There were always flowers in the vases though never in our part, but in the reception part of the convent, where the parents came. Their houses were houses of God and they attended them beautifully, particularly the church or chapel which was truly the tabernacle and the temple of God. It was so serene, so polished and so clean it had a profound effect on me and every room that I live in harks back to that spectacular way of housekeeping.

I think another positive side is that the nuns did impart a great respect for human life, a great respect for all the moral issues of life. They made you think very seriously about the question of chastity, about the question of sex. Whether it damaged you or not is another thing, but you had to think about it quite strongly. They made your sensibilities extremely tender, and though I think that's a bad weapon to enter life with, it's a valuable weapon if you're going to be an artist. They taught you the nature of love – in an odd sort of way they were very loving people although I really don't like their love. You can't spit on anybody's love, you can't say this isn't the form of love I want, but their love seems to me to be so misplaced and their love of God seems

to me to be so narrow. For me the love of God and the love
of life is much the same thing. It has to do with embracing
every aspect of it and trying to come to terms with the ugly,
of working out why these things should be, not turning your
back on them. I think my whole curious insecure search for
what is good and what is love and what is life has to do with
my observation of nuns trying to arrive at the same thing.
Because there is no doubt that the nuns by whom I was
educated, and with whom I lived during those very difficult,
damaging years were good women. They did their very best
in the true sense and in doing their very best they often did
the worst for the people in their charge – but they would be
grieved to think that. They couldn't think it because if they
did they would have to rethink their whole lives. Since their
whole lives were predicated on being virgins, on God literally being their lover, on being, that strange sexual
expression, 'the bride of Christ', how could they take on
board what I'm saying? I admire them in a strange way but
I want no part of them and I wouldn't get any of the pleasure that Irish mothers are supposed reputedly to get when
their son is a priest and their daughter's a nun.

I did not send my daughters to convent schools.
Adolescents suffer enough, have enough insecurities without
being told that there is a better way to live, quite openly,
easily accessible: 'Take the habit and enter the monastery.' I
didn't want them to have that. If they arrived at that decision in quite a different way, then that's something else. I
mean I know girls who have gone off to be nuns in their
thirties. That seems to me to be an acceptable thing to do,
to go into retirement when you have known the world, when

you have learned what the world is about, to decide that you don't want that part of it, that what you do want is quietness and contemplation. It may be an escape and a retreat – but it's a perfectly understandable one.

Frances Donnelly

Frances attended the Ursuline Convent, Wimbledon, London from 1957 to 1964. She is a journalist and mother of a teenage daughter. Her first novel *Shake Down the Stars* was published in 1988 and she is currently writing a third.

'Looking back, I can see that the nuns were essentially single women trying to cope with a very unruly set of girls who were awash with hormones.'

'The laughter of nuns is the sweetest sound.' I can remember when I heard that saying first. I was in my late teens, about seventeen or eighteen, and it struck an immediately discordant note. My immediate thought was: well, if you had three meals a day, free clothes and a bed for life without doing anything, you'd be laughing too. What irritated me about it was the fact that within the Catholic Church certain people, mainly men, needed to believe that there was one group of people who were happy, innocent and free ... in other words, didn't have sex. That seemed to me to be an extraordinarily bleak image of womanhood to offer teenage girls. It was an image that lay across your path like a felled tree. You didn't want to be like that but there weren't any other images around within the convent that you could relate to.

I always found the nuns a fairly mean-spirited, bigoted set of women who I felt wouldn't survive very well in the outside world. That's a judgement made in my teens when I was furious with the nuns because I didn't feel they answered my emotional needs. I never had any evidence of any kind of spiritual life. We attended church a lot and they attended church a lot but I never saw that permeating their judgement.

My grievances about the nuns do have some sort of

personal basis and the charge I make against them is that they lacked compassion. My mother died when I was fourteen years old. She died after a long protracted illness so everybody knew she was going to die, yet, from the day she died it was never mentioned again at the convent. Never, not a single word. My work was not brilliant at the best of times and we had that awful system whereby every fortnight your marks were read out and you were made to form lines of A minus, then B minus with the C minus where I was at the front. Reverend Mother would put on her glasses and have a really good look. I was doing so badly in class, and yet it was never related to the fact that I'd had a bereavement – in a sense the most shocking bereavement an adolescent girl can have.

Two days after my mother's funeral I truanted for the one and only time in my academic career. Did we go off and have a good time? No, we went to see *101 Dalmatians* at the cinema. The following day we were hauled out in front of the school and we had our house colours removed. We were given a terrible public roasting. It seems to me inconceivable that anyone with even an amateur knowledge of psychology would not have asked the question *why* was this girl truanting.

People get very excited about convent schools and imagine that all kinds of things go on. They don't. We lived a life of absolute unparalleled boredom. In my first year at school we all had crushes on the games mistress. By the time we got to the sixth form we quite rightly thought ourselves objects to be fantasised about by the upper thirds. Unfortunately they already had pictures of the Beatles inside their desks and were very keen on the idea of dating which we knew very little about. The nuns had absolutely no idea – we weren't given any formal sexual education at all. They knew about grooming you for a Catholic marriage, they knew about siphoning off a few to enter the order and they knew about getting the girls they could see, from the age of eleven, were likely to get pregnant, into the third stream.

You were given the idea by the nuns that sex, particularly sex in women, was a terrifying commodity. It certainly couldn't be controlled by women and it was safest held in marriage where the constant act of producing children would wear it out pretty quickly. They completely failed to grasp the idea that anybody would want to do anything sexually other than for the purpose of having children. One day we asked one of the nuns about French kissing. She brooded about this for a long time and finally said, 'It's all right if you put your tongue in a man's mouth a little way but *don't* make a meal of it.'

They made the whole idea of sex so fraught and fearful that I think we had it on our minds much more than girls at, say, an ordinary grammar school. It was a light switch and we never knew where it was. We were not in control of it . . . you might put your hand on it by mistake and set a World War in motion when all you wanted to do was find your way to the table.

When I was at school in the late 50s and early 60s there was a tremendous amount of snobbery. Women were preoccupied with not being 'common'. People lost sleep over 'being common' and there was a terrible finger of scorn: 'She looked rather common.' These were always the girls who did it and got pregnant and were no better than they should be. The nuns were very clear early on about separating the girls who they thought were a bit 'common' from the rest of us who had no charm at all and could safely be left on our own until the age of twenty-one, unmolested. The girls who were 'common' were put into cookery and were turning out cheese scones at twelve while the rest of us were wrestling with Latin verbs. The nuns had worked out how you could limit the damage and they did this by deciding which girls would make good wives and mothers earlier than the rest.

The religious teaching all got mixed up in a fudge in our heads. There are various grades of sin of which mortal sin is the worst. When you commit a mortal sin the soul dies and if you die after committing it you go straight to hell. No tribunal, no special plea bargaining, St Peter says, Off! So, we were often in a terrified state about being in mortal sin – mainly over things like impure thoughts or masturbation. I'm sure that's why so many Catholic girls go wrong because mortal sin was so awful, there was no way back, there was no God of compassion or understanding. The fact was, once you'd committed fornication, your soul was dead and therefore you could not receive communion which was a very significant thing. Once I'd done 'it' I knew I couldn't go to confession or Holy Communion anymore, unless I made up my mind to stop doing it. I stopped going to church altogether and fourteen years of very detailed, close religious education had just gone. Contrary to what the nuns feared for us we didn't want non-stop promiscuity and a good time with the rugby team. What we wanted was what we called a 'meaningful' relationship with the man of our choice and this meant we slept with him. We had put ourselves in a position where it was no longer worth going to Mass or to church anymore and that was the way we all lapsed.

I think the nuns found my generation threatening. They didn't know how the energy in a woman could be channelled other than into the roles of Catholic wife, mother or nun. I do think a Catholic education, as it was then, did make you opinionated but you learnt your opinions very painfully because they were resisted very strongly all the way. You had no sense of what was your right, what was your due, what your needs were. The ideal Catholic woman in my day was the mother who made herself into a doormat, threw herself on the ground and said, 'Walk over me folks – come on Daddy, come on you little children, especially you boys!' Her needs did not exist. She went on having more and more children and that was seen to be the full gamut of what a woman's needs ought to be. I resent that very much because it's taken me until now, in my forties, to say, 'Just a minute, I'm glad you're all having a good time, but what am I getting out of it?' Women are brought up to believe that those who give selflessly will be the best wives. For the sake of yourself you have to say, 'I have my rights too.' But that was nowhere in evidence in our convent education at all. We perceived fairly early on that the nuns didn't have any power. Priests have powers just the way doctors have powers and nurses don't. I've always noticed with both parties, nurses get terribly excited by the presence of doctors just as nuns get incredibly excited by the presence of a priest.

Invariably, at a dinner party, I can tell who's been to a convent and who hasn't. There's a style that comes simply from the great emphasis on manners and on being ladylike. At the time it was all mixed up in our heads with God and what God wanted. God appeared to me to be a rather waspish old gay up in heaven who was furious when people didn't wear white gloves. He got very uptight indeed and worried about finger bowls and things like that. So, we learned to be polite to each other and to behave politely in company which is no bad thing.

Looking back I can see that the nuns were essentially single women trying to cope with a very unruly set of girls who were awash with hormones. They did the best they could although we didn't find it very satisfactory at the time. They were women who perhaps weren't going to get married, whose parents weren't going to be able to afford any training for them. How else were they *not* going to be a burden to their families, how else were they going to make any life for themselves away from home?

I laughed at what the nuns said to us, yet I think in their own clumsy, inept and entirely unhelpful way they were trying to protect us. It was 1963 or 64 and they knew that there was no real effective method of contraception and that the perils and penalties for girls who stepped out of line were punitive – but not for the men who got them pregnant. I know girls who were at school with me and even though they married subsequently they have never got over what they were made to feel, not only by the nuns but by the Catholic community.

To fully appreciate the school I went to you'd have to go

back about a hundred years. Nowadays, I think convent schools seem to be good and caring and responsible and they understand that women have to take a proper place in the world. At the best kind of convent school I think there is a degree of caring, which you don't get at an ordinary school, simply because that is the nuns' whole life. But I didn't feel that at my school. They weren't helping us really to grow up and deal with life's problems. How could they? They knew nothing about them.

Marcella Evaristi

Marcella Evaristi, the daughter of Scottish-Italian parents, attended two convent schools in Glasgow, Mary Lea and Notre Dame in the 1960s. In 1983 she wrote the award-winning BBC play *Eve Set The Balls of Corruption Rolling*, a comedy about an old girls' reunion at a convent school. She lives in London with her son and her daughter.

'Somebody will say, "I was in hospital, had this operation and the nuns were marvellous, they were angels." And you can always tell the Catholics, they stiffen up because they remember this one bad bitch who made their lives a misery!'

The first thing I remember was the interminable prayer sessions first thing in the morning. They were so long that girls used to faint, fall like skittles – that was par for the course. You didn't think how extraordinary, somebody's fainted, as you would now. You thought: Oh, only three today ... Only in later life do you look back and think, gosh, that was weird!

I didn't consciously think of my primary school as being strict, it was just the extraordinary routine. A lot of stamina was needed for all those hours in church. It was *internalised* strict if you know what I mean. I do think there are certain advantages to children being given a kind of 'moral seriousness'. I think that's important. On the other hand, looking back with love at the person I was when I was eight or nine (and having children myself now) I really don't like the moral torture which that kind of violent belief can be to a child. As you get older you think life's too short, childhood is for being happy. You shouldn't actually be imagining that you're going to be tortured by the devil.

I do remember a kind of heady battle with the faith. I decided one night that I would really be good, I'd really pull out all the stops; I would astound the world with how good I was going to be. This seemed like a wonderful thing to try and do. Actually if you are logical about the religion, there is only one thing to try and be, and that is a saint.

Everything else is finite. So I was really determined to become the best girl that ever was in existence. Then I had these terrible dreams about the devil trying to tempt me. You see if you take on all that stuff so early the black side is that you can get a wee soul completely overtaken by it and in retrospect I think that is worrisome.

I suddenly realised what I was doing to get to sleep at night was actually a 'sin'. I was a very devout child so I thought: My God, this is awful. I've been taking communion and doing this terrible thing. I thought, I must confess this and I finally did, just as I put it in the play. I told the priest that I was unchaste, unchaste with myself. It was like a great burden of guilt being lifted off my shoulders, I felt wonderful. He said: 'Bless you, my *son.*' I thought, what do I do? Go back in the door and say, I'm sorry, I was just in before, I'm a girl, I've got pigtails you know. It's weird!

I remember at primary school there was one nun who'd been a missionary and she was very sweet and I absolutely adored her, fell in love with her, but the headmistress – she was bad. When you normally go to confession it's completely secret and that's the deal. For some reason I can't remember, maybe there was building work being done in the church, whatever – there were confessions in Sister Mary Clare's room. We were all lining up in the hall and we thought: Well, at least she won't be so vulgar and two-faced as to hang around. But she did hang around! There we were saying, 'Bless me Father for I have sinned . . .' and thinking: She's not gone out of the room. Well, that's not fair!

As far as sex education went, there wasn't much of it

around. I remember we got a little booklet but it was so unspecific. The way boys were 'sold' was that no matter what happened it was your fault. Basically, if you were raped by a gorilla it was your fault for wearing frosted-pink lipstick, you tart. It was the double sexual standard – squared! Lust was what boys felt, not girls, that was lesson number one. It was very pernicious in that sense and I would hate to think that my daughter was anywhere near that kind of feeling. With children their sexuality is so open at that stage, they're sensual beings, to force on them this idea that sexuality is something that boys have, that girls have the responsibility to control, seems to me like taking their childhood away as much as their sexuality.

One thing I do remember is that I was crazy about drama and wanted to go to drama school. We went to the headmistress because a friend and I wanted to start up a wee drama society in the school. There were music groups, debating societies and we wanted to set up a drama society. (Ideally what we wanted was to be at the RSC playing Juliet on alternate nights!) She told us we couldn't become actresses because unlike non-Catholic girls we couldn't use the casting couch. We hadn't a clue what she was talking about. That seemed to me loopy!

The other thing I remember about the headmistress was that she really didn't like Italians. I think she thought only Irish Catholics counted. Italian ones were a bit devious. She was only ever nice to the Italian girls just before there was a party or celebration or a parents' day. Because, of course, all the Italians had cafés, so she'd get free ice-cream. We could always tell when there was a parents' day coming up – suddenly the Jackanellis and the Evaristis starting getting treated nice. I know it's different now, but can you imagine the lunacy – all those little girls being educated by a group of women who had no experience of the world at all. They probably went from their father's house straight into the convent. It's not surprising that ideologically, emotionally and psychically they go askew. It'd be a miracle if they didn't.

What I do remember is the capitalism of convent schools. All these wee shops they have. They used to do an incredibly clever number where the week-girls in my convent had to wear a blue ribbon on their hair, even if their hair was short. So you'd get these wee souls with cropped hair with a big fat blue ribbon tied on to elastic and plomped on their hair. They looked bizarre. And you couldn't just use any blue ribbon, no, no, no, you had to buy it from the school. At vast profit.

There was also a little shop where you could buy holy pictures and they were all graded. I remember you could get your ordinary Immaculate medal or you could get your really super-duper one. With paint and twinkles on it. Looking back, I do think of it as a wee bit mean, the moments of anguish: Will I go into the tuck shop and buy a Mars bar or will I buy a holy picture for my mother? All right, holy picture. I used to buy ones with little bits of lace around them, very baroque, very rococo!

At Notre Dame, the secondary school I went to, there was a girl that I completely idolised. I thought she was wonderful. She knew all the Bob Dylan lyrics off by heart, she was really cool and she dyed her hair. She was so hip it

wasn't true. I wanted to aspire to this. Her name was Jackie
and Jackie was always getting into trouble because she was
a wild girl, a kind of Annie Lennox in uniform. There was
a train strike at Central Station and the queues around the
station were huge – front-page news in the *Glasgow Herald*
which carried a big picture. Jackie Hurley was right at the
front of the queue *and she had her hat off!* She was just holding
it. About ten ex-pupils had sent the photograph to Sister
Ann to say your standards at the school are going down. I
thought, oh God, Jackie's on the front page of the *Herald*
without her hat! Looking like she doesn't care, looking like
Bob Dylan. It was wonderful. My hero, Jackie! One of the
things I find a great compliment in a way about *Eve* is that
I got so many letters from all over the country, England as
well as Scotland, convinced that it was *their* school. It makes
you feel you must have touched something there somewhere.

I think it's a better idea to write plays about going back
and never go back in reality. I never actually did go to any
reunions at all. I think that the process of a writer anyway is
'a going back'. You must have a special kind of memory to
be a writer and therefore it struck me as a good idea for a
piece, to recreate that sense of what we were like then, what
we're like now.

The spine of the play is a character who at school was
much put down because there was a lot of petit bourgeois
snobbery. The character is illegitimate and everybody else
seems to have 'a better set-up'. What happens is that her
father leaves her money and she has this hotel in Skye. She
comes back with the Porsche and the fur, determined to

make everybody green with jealousy. What they're actually all doing is saying, 'How's Brendan at nursery school?' and, 'Oh, my car got scratched last week . . . .' Nobody actually cares that much. She comes back with this sense of class revenge and nobody's listening! She gets pissed and she completely screws it basically. The most fatal thing you can do at a reunion is to go back to prove yourself. You should go back for a laugh, for curiosity, to hit somebody on the chin even, but not *ever* to prove yourself. I think that must be the most fatal, self-destructive thing you can do. One auto-biographical truth was that the actual school I went to was a direct grant school and it was academically very good, but it wasn't actually that posh. But when it finally went comprehensive there was a certain strand of snobbery from girls who'd gone to the school, who felt liberated to recreate it in their imagination as some kind of Roedean that had become an inner city ghetto comprehensive. Neither of these things were true. In fact the school is academically just as good as it ever was. The only thing now is that the girls are allowed to wear anoraks and they don't have to wear the uniform, they don't have to wear the hat. It struck me as something about the nature of memory, that if something has changed irrevocably you were then free to fantasise about what had happened before.

You're either a good writer or a bad writer and whatever has happened to you, you'll use it, but what I certainly think is true about being a Catholic is that when the experience is that vivid it makes for good copy. It is difficult to say what you would have been with a different kind of background – I mean Italian Protestants are thin on the ground! If I was really to analyse it I think it is quite baroque as copy. The imagery is strong and for a writer that's important.

When I was asked for pictures [for the TV programme] I went up to our wee attic with my mother to look at the old photographs, which I must say I did with a certain tenderness, rather than with any feelings of real discomfort. I think the kind of discomfort that would have really killed somebody like me off was the appalling English boarding school tradition, of sending little ones off to strangers when they're seven – that's a hellish background. What I had was a mishmash of the lyrical and the ignorant. It's just become part of my bones now. It's like a stain on your psyche, it's the colour you are. I think it'd be impossible to exorcise it from yourself.

Who would choose *not* to be a Catholic if they could? It would be much nicer to believe. Instead of which I think that when I die I'll never see my children again, I'll never see my loved ones again. Whereas if you had the faith you would believe that this is just a bad technical rehearsal and the real thing is going to be in Jesus' arms forever. Who would choose to be like Shaw says, 'Man is a genius, tethered to a dying animal.' I'm not a Catholic anymore. I'm saying that I'd like to believe it, it would be lovely to believe that we are not finite. Sadly, I think that we are and I think that when you go, you go. I would prefer to believe differently, but I can't force myself to.

Who can tell the effect of your past on your present? I don't know and it's a difficult one because I am ambivalent about it. Having children myself I wish you could prise out the good bits from the bad bits. I haven't had my children baptised, which was a very difficult decision to make, because I don't have the faith anymore and it would have been hypocritical of me to use a sacrament as a piece of social frippery. I want them baptised as lapsed Catholics, but there isn't the ritual! Then I'd be comfy, we'd all be the same in the same house, which is what one aspires to.

Germaine Greer

Writer and teacher, Germaine Greer won a scholarship to the Star of the Sea Convent, Gardenvale, Victoria, Australia and was educated by the Presentation nuns from 1952 to 1955. She attended universities in Melbourne, Sydney and Cambridge and wrote her first book *The Female Eunuch* in 1970. She is now Professor of English and Comparative Studies at the University of Warwick.

'I think one of the reasons I was never properly domesticated is because I was actually socialised by a gang of mad women in flapping black habits.'

My father married my mother in a Catholic Church so he had to make a promise that I'd be brought up in my mother's religion. That was ironic seeing as she didn't even observe it, but I think she knew that the convent would give me a better education. My father, on the other hand, always believed I was taught badly. Week in, week out, I had to take it from him that I was going to an inferior school. In fact, it turns out that he was barely literate himself and had a very poor education – it was a piece of anti-catholic prejudice. Even when I won a scholarship to university my father did not revise his opinion. The scholarships were graded in order of merit for the whole state; I was second in the state and the girl who sat next to me was first. Bigotry really doesn't listen to any kind of evidence at all. I realise now I had a terrific education.

At the time, The Star of the Sea Convent seemed to me a very big, forbidding, grey Gothic building with a tarmac yard like a prisoners' exercise yard. Of course when I went back there seventeen years later it was just a little place, a sweet, little school.

I remember all the nuns vividly. There was Sister Raymond who taught me about art. She had big round bosoms and big round hips and she loved art even though she'd never seen any. She'd never seen anything. Yet she used to stand there pointing to these pictures saying: 'Look at it, it's beautiful! Oh, look it's really beautiful!' I sometimes wonder what it would be like if I took her with me round Europe and said: 'You remember, you taught me about Chartres. Well this is Chartres and this is what it looks like.' And Durham. Every time I go there I can hear that voice saying: Look! It's beautiful!

Then there was Sister Cyril who taught us French and who was very frail and rather sensual and feminine. When men came into the room to do things like mend the window catch she used to practically writhe herself into conniptions. We decided she was a pretty sad case.

There was Sister Philip who taught us Chemistry and who I remember because I hit her with a softball straight into the front of her coif, which crumpled it and knocked her flat. I remember everyone. Sister Michael who taught me German and who had a face that looked as if it had been scrubbed hard with steel wool. And Sister Attracta, who taught us singing. I'll always remember Sister Attracta. She really did wonders with us. I sang three or four times a week in a madrigal choir. We sang Masses, we sang operetta, we sang everything. I'm still singing the same things, thirty-five years later.

I especially remember Sister Eymard who tried to teach me the philosophical proofs of the existence of God, and thereby destroyed my faith completely because she didn't know them. Rather, she did know them but they weren't valid. She was always in a hurry – the sort of nun who would go through a room rearranging all the furniture with her habit. There was one room in the convent where we were never allowed to go – the parlour – unless it was very important. For some reason I was waiting in there one day when I heard an enormous crash outside in the corridor. I opened the door and peeped out and there was Sister Eymard on her back having skidded on the drugget down the middle of the corridor. All I know was that I was not to go and pick her up; I was to shut the door very quietly and just go back and sit on the horsehair sofa until somebody came. Poor Sister Eymard. In the end she got run over, probably because she was charging across the road without looking.

I think one of the reasons why I was never properly domesticated is because I was actually socialised by a gang of mad women in flapping black habits. I'm more like them than I am like my mother. I owe them more in a way because they loved me more and they worked harder on me than my mother did. They really loved us. I realise that now, although I didn't realise it at the time.

They were very excited to have such a clever little girl in the school and anything I did was all right with them. I was forgiven within two seconds because I'd say something funny or clever. They brought out the best in me and it needn't have been brought out, it could have stayed right where it was. I could have married a stock-broker and settled into a life of three cars and a carport. They made that impossible because I was hungry for something else – spiritual values. Just not *their* spiritual values.

I was always in trouble but I always came bouncing back for more. The nuns used to say I took correction beautifully, but then they gave correction beautifully. Having been a teacher myself it was the orderliness of the school that impressed me most. The calm, and the fact that we were disciplined in soft voices. The worse the trouble you were in, the softer the voice. They'd deliver this rabbit killer punch in a soft, soft voice. If you were being really rambunctious and a pain in the neck you'd be asked to leave the room. You'd be standing outside the room, thinking: Oh God, it was pretty boring in there, but it's much more boring out here. Every time, along would come Reverend Mother, the silent padding presence in the corridor. She'd come silently down the corridor just looking for someone like me and say: 'Well Germaine? What's the trouble?' And I'd say: 'Oh, I said I didn't think Communism was the work of the devil.' And she'd say 'Oh, Germaine, you could be a great saint or a great sinner. The choice is entirely up to you.' I'd be thinking: 'great sinner, great sinner!'

I think all girls' schools are fairly hysterical institutions. I'm very fond of women in groups. I want to see women being happier in their groups and less apologetic for them. I like the way women laugh without self-consciousness when there are no men around. If you go into a pub you won't hear women rolling on the floor with laughter. You'll hear the polite responses to men's jokes. You won't hear too many jokes by women either, because they're watching someone else's performance. When you're within convent walls or college walls then the women's innate creativity has to come out. So, we were uproarious and the nuns were uproarious too. They were all droll and mad in their particular ways. They didn't conform to any stereotype, they were all different.

People always think that nuns are nuns because they're

disappointed in love. Wrong. Nuns are nuns usually because they are in love. They're just in love with Somebody we don't know too much about. He's called Christ and He really is the archetypal lover. They love him in a way which is deeply passionate and has a lot of referred emotion stored up in it. We all went through that phase. When I was fifteen, I was regularly taken up unconscious from the floor of the church because I'd go there and kneel with my arms stretched out for hours on end, making love to this image . . . this person really.

The one thing the nuns don't do is take sex for granted, or trivialise it or turn it into a sport. For all convent girls sex is hugely attractive, dark, mysterious and very powerful. I hesitate to suggest for one moment that the tabloid press is perceptive, but I think convent girls do have a special kind of intensity, a special kind of physical awareness. The nuns wanted us to know that sex was something very powerful that you fooled with at your peril. They convinced us that our bodies were just charged with this amazing stuff and if we did so much as bare the top part of our arms, we could be an occasion of sin. It could cause lascivious thoughts to come into somebody's head. I think they were too innocent to realise that there are a lot of men out there who have lascivious thoughts when they see school uniforms. They thought the school uniform was the armour of chastity. It was only when we got dressed up in our ghastly frocks for the ball and dances that they would fill our fronts with Kleenex in case a taller boy should peer down them. I was already six feet tall and there wasn't a boy in the room who was going to see down that cleavage.

I did think that sex was something extremely powerful and holy, to be approached with great trepidation. It's been an ongoing disappointment in my life to discover that other people don't give it that much importance. I really expected the stars to shoot from their spheres when I finally undid more than one button. We were all sex-struck and that's the nuns' fault entirely.

When I left school I was faced with this ghastly thing called dating. I didn't know what the hell it was supposed to be about. All I knew was that as soon as you went anywhere with a young man, whether he paid for the tickets or not, he was all over you, putting all kinds of pressure on you. I just decided that dating was the pits and that was my convent training. It just said: Look, by all means, if you want to make love to a man, do it and take the consequences, but this ignoble business of groping and finger-fucking, keep out of it. It's vile and it's called hypocrisy. It's no use being a demivierge; you have to be either fiercely virginal or fiercely non-virginal.

I remember arguing with a girlfriend of mine who was boasting about how her boyfriend used to burst into tears and beat his head against the steering wheel when she was teasing him. I remember saying to her: 'You're worse than a prostitute.' That was the end of our relationship but I refused to be what was called a 'cock-teaser'. So, I began attacking that cold-blooded, exploitative system of dating and necking and petting. I found the whole thing disgusting and, frankly, I couldn't do it. I was either too passionate or too cold. I either wasn't coming on enough or I was coming on for something. I'd get it wrong all the time. I began arguing against sexual guilt and hypocrisy while I was still a virgin. I mean that's a very nun-like thing to do!

In *The Female Eunuch* I said, eschewing the company of men is not the point because convents have been around a long time and they've done very little to liberate women. My attitude to that has changed to some extent. I do think there's a lot to be said for segregation. The more I look at segregated societies in different countries, the more it seems to me that women actually have a more satisfactory life when they're less dependent upon a single man. What makes women so desperate in our society is that without 'the man' who legitimates their whole existence they can't really survive. They think that just going out to dinner with the girls is something awful. I mean why? Men don't think that going out to dinner with the blokes is somehow awful. So why have women got themselves into this situation, especially as I believe women haven't got much in common with men? Constant consorting with men is very alienating for women eventually. Women discover this at menopause if they don't discover it before. At menopause they suddenly become completely invisible to the people they've spent their whole lives truckling to.

The Female Eunuch was written by a thirty-year-old sexually active woman who insisted on the right to make her own choices. If she wanted five hundred sexual partners, that's what she was going to have and if she wanted one, or none, that's what she was going to have. I haven't changed my views on that at all. I am still saddened by the fact that women are so powerless in the sex situation. They've got no bargaining power at all. Young women today are still just as emotionally vulnerable as they ever were. It's still much more important to them than it is to the chaps and as long as that situation exists, women's self-esteem takes a terrible knocking if they don't achieve something like a relationship.

On the question of religion, I think it is important to separate Catholicism from conventism. To be a Catholic is one thing. To be a convent girl is another. You might not even be a very good Catholic because the nuns were dreadfully incompetent at teaching Catholic philosophy. The Jesuits on the other hand are very good at it, and if I'd been taught by Jesuits I'd probably still be a Catholic. But I was taught by nuns and they blew it. It's as simple as that.

All the time I went to confession I confessed things that weren't sins because the nuns had given me the idea that they were. I'd say: 'Bless me Father for I have sinned, I have missed my morning and night prayers, Father.' That's not a sin. The nuns said it was a sin of omission but I don't think it is. I used to get annoyed when I was a kid and say to them: 'You make Heaven sound like banking! If I get enough credits, I've got all this stuff in Heaven and I can even lend it out to other people.' I quite like the idea of praying for other people, though. I don't think Protestants have ever understood about Indulgences, that you can get Indulgences for other people and that's what you spend most of your life doing. There is an attempt to grade sins according to their gravity, but the order they get them in is pretty rotten. One has the distinct impression that sex is worse than stealing or lying or violence or cruelty.

I am still a Catholic, I just don't believe in God. I am an

atheist Catholic – there's a lot of them around. I don't want to escape from it, I'm very glad to be Catholic. Very often, when Jehovah's Witnesses and all those people come round to make a nuisance of themselves, I open the door and say: 'This is a Catholic household.' Which it is. At least it was; at one time we were all lapsed Catholics in the house. One thing lapsed Catholics don't do is go in for an 'inferior' religion with less in the way of tradition and intellectual content. So, when the vicar comes round and tries to enlist my aid for the building fund of the Protestant church in the village, I say: I'm a Catholic.

I think the worst problem now in convent schools is that there are so few nuns and so many lay teachers. I don't think it makes that much difference that the nuns have left off their habits although I think they were beautiful, really elegant. The nylon frocks with the double welted seams and lisle stockings are grim by comparison. I loved the way the nuns looked and they loved the way they looked as well. They had to love the habit, that was part of the rule of the order. Lots of old nuns still wear the wimple even though they don't have to now.

One of the most important things about going to a convent is that they don't lock the place up at four-thirty and disappear, let alone not do playground duty or not look after children on their way to the bus stop. The nuns made sure that we were taken care of all the time. There was always somebody there. There was always somebody watching over us so we couldn't get up to vicious games in the playground. I pity the drug pedlar in a convent school. The nuns would have seen it in an instant. I think if you actually look at statistics you will see, even in the inner city, nuns are attacked by school children less often than other teachers; that their decibel level in the classroom is lower; and that the children are looked after in a more comprehensive way. They have a commitment that goes way beyond wages. They struggled with all of us to do the best with us that they could. No girl from our school was in trouble with the police and not a girl from our school would have been abandoned by the nuns if she was. They would have made sure that there was some other outcome.

I'm sure the nuns would much rather I had a change of heart and became a great Catholic polemicist and was as noisy about Catholicism as I have been about everything else. I don't really think there's much chance of that, although the nuns will be praying for it. That's the worst thing about the blessed nuns, they're praying for you, hell for leather, every day. This gang of Presentation nuns are going to haul me up to Heaven whether I like it or not!

When I was at school the nuns got an allowance for basic bodily necessities which included sanitary napkins, soap and hair pins. They got fifteen shillings a week. They had no money because of their vow of poverty, yet the Australian education system would have collapsed without the exploitation of this group of women. Having said that, they generally lived in nicer houses with gardens and ate better food than the average single woman teacher could ever manage. Their communal life did make for a good lifestyle with good conversation, good books, lots of travelling from one house to another and lots of time for contemplation. I think it's a good life. I just wish it hadn't lost so much of its inner justification. As long as it is done out of passionate love for Our Lord, it can't be regarded as simply oppressive. For many centuries the convent was the only way out of oppressive marriages and they were often very epicurean places where nuns made great music, put on plays and saw the best of everything.

There's no reason why it shouldn't be like that again. People ask me what I want my house to be like. I usually say I would like it to be like the abbey of Thélème in Rabelais, the secular nunnery, where all kinds of elaborate pleasures are constructed and enjoyed. I think there's something to be said for nunneries. I'm not sure that there's anything to be said for Catholicism. That's the problem.

Alison Halford

Although she was not a Roman Catholic at the time, Alison Halford attended the Notre Dame Convent School in Norwich from 1945 to 1956. She later joined the Metropolitan Police in London and went on to become Assistant Chief Constable in Merseyside, which made her Britain's highest ranking woman police officer. Denied further promotion, Alison's career terminated after her sex discrimination case against her chief constable and the Home Secretary was settled. In 1995 she stood successfully as a Flintshire County Councillor and in 1999 was elected to serve as an Assembly member to the National Assembly for Wales. She was one of the first 60 people to participate in the first historic self-government of Wales.

Alison, who converted to Catholicism in 1963, worships regularly with the sisters of the Convent of the Poor Clares in Hawarden.

'One episode that I do remember brought a letter from the head teacher to my parents. I had been eating a lollypop, of all things, in school uniform in the street – and that really was almost a hanging job!'

There were two good schools in Norwich and my parents chose Notre Dame, I suppose because they wanted to make sure that I was brought up a lady with a good education. The nuns were known to impart those sort of skills. They set very high standards, with a lot of emphasis on good academic ability and they worked hard to make sure that you did excel in all things. I was one of those late starters so if you go back to the school you won't find my name on many boards of excellence.

Although some of the nuns were rather forbidding the majority of them were very kind, caring, loving people. There was a good mix of nuns and lay teachers; it was a very friendly school, a compassionate school where they worked you hard, set high standards, but it was a very nice place to be in.

It was a very big old convent with wide corridors and beautiful polished parquet floors. There was always the smell of polish and, because the food was cooked on the premises, the smell of cabbage was always in my nostrils. And from the chapel wafted the smell of candles burning and occasionally incense.

The teacher I remember best was Miss Fowler, quite an eccentric lady, who went under the affectionate nickname of 'Chicken'. She was the PE mistress and she had a most peculiar shape – a lot in the front and a lot behind with very short muscular legs. But she was an absolute sweetie and she was about the one person who could see that I might make something of my life. I was always the leader who led everybody astray, always the unwitting rebel, and she would say, 'Alison, I think you will make something of your life, you will end up as a prime minister or something like that.' I thought – Wowee! Somebody does recognise my talents ... So I have a very fond memory of Miss Fowler.

I surprised myself and everybody else when I was eleven by winning a handwriting competition. I remember this because I never won anything else. I remember the nun announcing, 'Now we've got the winner of the handwriting competition and guess who it is ...'

They tried to guess – and there was nobody left in the class apart from me. My secretary would laugh her socks off if she knew because my handwriting now is so appalling.

There were one or two unfortunate incidents I remember. It was a very large school, with beautiful grounds, and the hay was cut and tied into bundles. I was messing around with a candle and trying to darken a glass to look at the sun, but something went wrong. The hay started smouldering, which of course caused a bit of a furore, and I was asked why I had done it. I said that it had been an accident and that I hadn't been on my own. To my extreme embarrassment (and this is where my early lying really caught me out) the whole school was asked to parade in front of me so that I could pick out the one who had allegedly helped me set fire to this bale of hay. An association with an identification parade so early in my life was quite significant. I didn't pick anybody out, I couldn't blame anybody when it wasn't their fault, so I sort of 'took the rap' on my own on that occasion. Another time which was really significant was when I carved my initials on the dining room table. That was rather a stupid thing to do because obviously I left a clue. The Sisters were not impressed with that at all and as a punishment I had to eat my meals cross legged on the floor for three days while all the rest of the eaters trooped past me. That was a lesson learned but I continued to be quite a rebel in my own way.

I had one of those joke button-holes – dried flowers you wore in your lapel, attached to a thin tube leading to a small squeezy water container you kept in your pocket. I must have been out of my mind on that particular day because I asked the maths teacher, a very formidable lady, 'Would you like to smell my button-hole?' – and then gave her a squirt. The aim was deadly and it caught her right in the eye! She was furious, took my beautiful device away from me and I never got it back again, so that was another lesson learned. Poor Miss Holmes.

I think I was quite a worry to them. The final episode that I do remember, in fact, brought a letter from the head teacher to my parents. I had been eating a lollypop, of all things, *in* school uniform *in* the street – and that really was almost a hanging job! Somebody saw me and I was reported to the teachers and that did end up with a very stern letter. So I learned not to eat sweeties in the streets.

I still don't understand quite how it works, but you can have lots of children all doing something and just one will get caught. I was always that one! The one time I played hookie I bumped into my form mistress. I would be the child whispering in class along with everybody else, but I would be the one sent out. Of course if you were sent out you then waited in fear and trepidation for the headmistress to walk round and catch you, and then of course you would be for the high jump all over again. To some extent, the fact that I was caught and maybe punished unnecessarily has gone towards making sure I think justice is important, that people shouldn't be accused and punished for things they haven't done. I am not saying that I wasn't guilty – I was just unfortunate to be caught all the time!

I think I have a heightened sense of justice. Clearly morals, good behaviour, proper standards, treating people properly were part of the school curricula. Whether that actually helped direct me into a police career I don't know, but there must be a connection between the two: a very good education with proper standards and wanting to come into a job which is all about treating people fairly and being decent to the community that you serve.

I think we all rebel at some stage in our lives – earlier or later, it doesn't really matter. But I do think it is important that you test the system at an early enough stage so that the system can't jump back and bite you. I mean if I had ended up with a criminal conviction, or something like that, I would not have been eligible for the police force. The fact that I did some silly things at school made me realise early on that there is authority, rules do have to be obeyed. Clearly that has been helpful for the career I have chosen.

I became interested in joining the police force when I was invited to go to the yearly police concert. I hadn't particularly wanted to go, but it would have been churlish to have refused. So I went and after talking to some police officers it sounded like an interesting career. Then I wandered along to Scotland Yard with a view to finding out more about the job and spoke to a very senior lady who wasn't actually able to tell me very much about the sort of hands-on experience. All I can recall was that she told me you can take away people's liberty and you have power of arrest! Police forces spend a lot of time checking on your references so therefore the challenge was laid down, could I actually get in? I was told years later that I was almost not accepted because I rolled up at the interview with green tips in my hair, which happened to be in vogue at the time. They thought I would be too flighty, far too interested in the fellas ever to make a career in the police service. Fortunately some member of the interview panel saw through the alleged flightiness and the green hair.

At school there was always a lot of emphasis on how you looked, particularly in uniform; kindness to people, being part of a team. Again emphasis was placed on raising money for charity, having to sell raffle tickets, Black Baby Day, being kind, caring and helpful. These were the important attributes and a great deal of emphasis was placed on these things.

In November there was always a big church bazaar and we worked hard to produce homemade goods which were sold to raise funds for the Black babies in Africa. Don't ask me where the money went but, somehow it was sent off to the African missionaries. I hope that's not seen as a racist statement now? Overall it was a very harmonious and happy atmosphere. A good clean hang-up-your satchel, put-away-your-shoes sort of environment.

In Liverpool unfortunately I see a lot of young people who have seriously lost their way, and I sometimes wonder what could have been done. Miss Fowler's words of encouragement have stayed in my memory for a long time and there were other teachers who were encouraging, as well as the supportive nuns. All that makes you feel valued and cherished and important – and that in turn makes you want to do something with your life. I think some of these elements are lacking in our current education for various reasons.

Patricia Hayes

Actress Patricia Hayes was born in 1909. She attended St Andrews Convent, Coventry Hall, Streatham in south London as a day pupil from the age of five to sixteen, after which she transferred to the Convent of the Sacred Heart in Wandsworth. She began appearing on stage from the age of twelve and never looked back. Her most celebrated television role was as *Edna, The Inebriate Woman* in the 1970s. She died in 1998, aged 88.

'It was only when I'd left drama school and gone into digs and was working for a repertory company that I read a book about the facts of procreation.'

My first convent was very strict. It was an order of Belgian nuns called the Dames de St André and ours was their only convent in England. When I was twelve I got my first professional stage engagement; for this you needed a licence in those days, and a letter from your school. My mother was too cowardly to go herself so she sent me. I was horrified. She said: 'Go to the school, knock on the front door, ask to see Reverend Mother and hand her this letter.' We were all rather frightened of these particular nuns.

When I was sixteen the nuns realised that my mother was determined that I should be an actress, so they asked her to take me away. They said: 'If Patricia is going to be an actress, she can't possibly have a good influence on the other girls here.' The Sacred Heart nuns with whom I completed my education were completely different. My mother, who was a bit of a snob, used to say it was because they were 'ladies'. She'd say: 'You can't *be* a Sacred Heart nun unless you're a lady. Some of the Belgian nuns are not exactly common, but they're suburban.' And it's true, some of them were!

The Sacred Heart was wonderful. I went to school in the mornings and to RADA in the afternoons. The headmistress Mother Burnett asked me to put on the school play – it was a completely different attitude. Their attitude was: Well a good Catholic girl, let her loose on the stage and she'll do nothing but good. The Belgian nuns thought I would be contaminated and led into a life of sin!

You have to remember that at the time, not only nuns but many people were very Victorian in their attitudes. My sister-in-law told me a true story about her own mother who was playing golf with a woman friend. It was about the time that all the scandal broke about the Prince of Wales and Mrs Simpson. Her mother said to the friend: 'What do you think about all this?' And the friend replied: 'Look, I'm sorry, but my husband has forbidden me to discuss it.' That was a middle-aged married woman whose husband found it so shocking that the heir to the throne could be involved in a divorce that he forbade his wife even to speak of it.

There was no sex education at any schools in those days. I think the nuns' attitude was that your parents should tell you what they thought was good for you to know. So I knew nothing. It was only when I'd left drama school and gone into digs and was working for a repertory company that I read a book about the facts of procreation. That was how I found out. I knew that babies came out of their mothers' tummies, but I thought they came out through the navel, and I had no idea how they got there in the first place.

Nuns had enormous respect for your parents. I remember once being told in class that it was a sin to sew on Sundays. 'Sundays should be devoted to prayer.' I went home and told my father what the nuns had said, and his response was: 'How can it possibly be a sin for an eight-year-old child to sew her dolls' dresses on a Sunday?' I went back to school and told the nun who just said: 'Well, if that's what your father says you must obey him. It's not for me, or you, to overrule what your father says.' They were always dreadfully pro men. And there was no creature on earth so wonderful as a priest. Yet, if you talked to a priest about the nuns, he'd invariably say: 'Oh, the nuns, take no notice of them.' It was rather like doctors and nurses!

I was a good child at school. In fact, I got a letter of rec-ommendation from the Reverend Mother saying my conduct was exemplary! I cried many times because I was often late for school. My mother was out at work, and most of the girls' mothers at a fee-paying school didn't go to work in those days. Mine did – she was a teacher and we needed the money. We were really hard up with three children to provide for. She didn't resign until I was fourteen. Then she was home for six months and bored out of her mind. So she went back to teaching.

I'm sort of against women with young children working really. I don't think there is anything better than a mother or a mother-figure at home when you come back from school. I was lucky. As an actress you only work some of the time and I got into a programme called 'Raise a Laugh' which I was in for five-and-a-half years. It had so many repeats that I could earn enough money to keep myself and my three children and only be out of the house one half day a week.

In most convents then the academic standards were not very good. They were very good on Religion and excellent on English grammar. My mother, being a teacher in a Catholic elementary school used to criticise the nuns, even on Religion. She had all the doctrine at her fingertips – she was absolutely spot on with everything. So, naturally, I came out first in RE. In a way I got Catholicism from all sides.

My father was not a Catholic, he was an Irish Protestant from the south of Ireland. I'm quite glad he wasn't a Catholic, because he was such a wonderful person and it did show me that you didn't have to be a Catholic to be a saint. Otherwise you could think that only Catholics are good. He was Protestant but very pro-Catholic in his ideas. I don't think he ever came out with any statement that a Catholic priest would have disagreed with. We would be taken to Mass while on holiday in Eire and I remember some nuns coming up to us and asking if we were Catholics. I said, 'Yes. Mummy is a Catholic, Daddy is not.' And she said, 'We must all pray that your father will become a Catholic.' And I said to her, 'My father is absolutely perfect the way he is.' And she said, 'Very well then, our prayer will be, thank God Patricia's daddy is such a wonderfully good man.'

The most useful thing I gained from my convent days was the acceptance that there has to be discipline. I remember one day a nun said to me: 'You are an extraordinary girl, Patricia. You don't do any work. You could be top of the class quite easily if you worked, but you don't. You choose not to work.' That really hit home and I set to work straight away. I think if you learn the value of work in any capacity, whether it's housework, gardening or anything, you have learnt something that stands you in good stead for the rest of your life. I would say at least eighty per cent of happiness is caused by the ability to enjoy work. Work is not a dirty word – to me it is God's most wonderful gift. If I sat doing nothing, my mother would say, 'Satan finds a lot of work for idle hands to do.' She was fond of those Victorian proverbs. But there should always be praise for achievement, even if it's only self-praise. I don't think we get enough praise and in my youth it was not thought to be good to praise children.

I was not aware of the 'sexy convent schoolgirl' idea in my school days. There are some girls who are sexy early on and there are some who are not. If a girl goes to a convent and is sexy people put the two together.

When I was in my forties I happened to meet some nuns from my first school once, quite by chance. They'd left Streatham and I met them in a country lane out at Edenbridge. I spoke to them and said: 'You know, you were much too old-fashioned.' And they agreed! When you're a parent nuns treat you quite differently from how they treated you as a child. As a child you're supposed to be respectful and not argue. I still think of the Sacred Heart nuns with enormous affection and appreciation. Some of them were absolutely wonderful and had such a sense of humour. I went back to an old girls' reunion and one of the nuns said to me: 'I must rush now, otherwise I'll miss my turn for a bath and the water will be cold.' I said to her: 'Mother, I didn't think nuns were allowed to talk about baths!' She laughed and said, 'You naughty girl.' They are lovely people really and they're enormously proud of me. I'm just as proud of them for being proud of me!

Convents have changed a lot since I was at school. They've had to. I was amazed when my older daughter went to the Sacred Heart Convent in Hammersmith and the nuns said to us: 'We teach them the facts of life. They learn it in biology. And furthermore we say, now you've got all that down in your exercise books, you must take it home tonight and show it to your parents, so that they know what you are being taught. There's no need for them to treat you as though you don't know, nor as though you *shouldn't* know.' These changes were bound to happen, but with convents things move more slowly. I think in many ways everything is better although we still have a lot of under-privileged people in our society. It is just a great pity that everybody can't have a really good education. Where would Mrs Thatcher be if she hadn't had one?

When I was at school, we knew the whole Catechism from beginning to end. We were taught it. I remember it extremely well. I can remember things I learnt as a child and yet I can't remember what I learned last week! We all had so many sections to learn each day and you would be heard saying your Catechism: Who made you? God made me. Why did God make you? God made me to know Him, love Him and serve Him in this life and to be happy with Him forever in the next. And you firmly believed that. Then it said: How many persons are there in God? There are three persons in God – the Father, the Son, the Holy Ghost. Are these three persons three Gods? These three persons are *not* three Gods. They are all one and the same God ... They don't use the Catechism now; I think that's a shame.

Sarah Hogg

Sarah Hogg was the second generation of her family to attend St Mary's, Ascot, one of Britain's most successful boarding schools, formerly run by nuns of the Institute of the Blessed Virgin Mary. According to her old headmistress, Sister Bridget, Sarah was quite a rebel but she was nevertheless made headgirl in her final year. Today she is chairman of 3i, Europe's leading venture capital company and the only woman to chair a company in the FTSE 100. She is director of three other companies, a Governor of the BBC and was made a Life Peer in recognition of her work in Downing Street in the 1990s. Sarah is married to MP Douglas Hogg. They have two children. Sarah's daughter also attended St Mary's and Sarah is a trustee of the school.

'This was a place that wasn't just a collection of women trying to get information into a bunch of teenagers, but it was a community that had the whole of life right through, including death, to deal with.'

There is a quality of unstated feminism at St Mary's. Most of the nuns would be horrified to hear me say that but I mean feminism in the best sense, which is a sense of woman's worth. If you join a community of women you must think that there is something special and important about doing so and this Order had that from the very beginning. Its history dates back about four centuries and it was founded by a Yorkshire woman, Mary Ward, who fought very hard for the right of a community of women to govern themselves, *not* to be governed by the Bishop. That was very important from the beginning, though it is taken for granted now, and there is no sort of positive feminism involved there. What was also important was the sense of community that comes from a convent school that is both people's home and their dedication, their dedication being twofold: the process of education and creating a community that consists of adolescent girls and women of all ages.

There was a great feeling for tradition when I was here. For instance, we had three different kinds of veil to wear, black for every day, white for Sundays, and a great big stiff white veil for feast days, but that has gone and to my mind it is a good thing because although theatricality is important in everyone's life, these things can get in the way of what is really here. Pare it down and the essence of the community is what comes through. Some sense of theatricality especially in the beautiful services I find very important, but none of the fringe trimmings that people think of as involved in convent education. What we still have is a beautiful chapel, and a lot of attention is paid to singing, to glorious performance, but it is not too pervasive as I think it was back in the sixties.

We were woken up in Latin every morning. A nun would come in and say, '*Benedicamus Domino*' and we were supposed to answer, '*Deo gratias*.' The correct answer came out about one time in ten. Latin was still the language of the Mass, and we said grace in Latin.

Then we started with Mass every morning; a church service was not unusual of course in any boarding school. It was in no sense an assembly, it was the Mass pure and simple. By the time my daughter got there things had changed considerably in that they went to Mass in the morning at will, not as a formal part of the process.

My mother was at the school too and her reaction to my descriptions was always, 'Hasn't it changed!' although I do think this process of change has been more rapid over the last twenty years. It seems to me most of the changes in the details of life here are for the better – though if ever the nuns depart completely an enormous amount will be lost.

I went from St Mary's pretty well straight to university, to a girls' college, so there was a kind of continuity. The process of being an adolescent is so dominant in one's thoughts that what's happening externally, in terms of where you are, is almost of secondary order. I think I was probably a very tiresome adolescent. I just got through it as best I could. It's a time when you become too concerned with yourself, too anxious about yourself, too extreme in your emotions, happy or unhappy. I think for that reason I was very lucky to have a convent education, though at the time I spent a lot of energy reacting against it in some way. I didn't feel any great change from school to outside.

One of my clearest memories is when Reverend Mother died. She was a great Reverend Mother, of enormous strength, the sort of character who, in the outside world, would have achieved an important position, but within a community was known only to us. When she died she was laid out with flowers and candles and we all filed past and said a prayer, two hundred of us. We were giggling thirteen-year-olds and we had never seen a dead body before. We went past and, of course, we found, as everyone does in those circumstances, that dead bodies aren't at all frightening. It left me with an image of continuity, because this was a place that wasn't just a collection of women trying to get information into a bunch of teenagers, but it was a community that had the whole of life right through, including death, to deal with. It is a very important image and I can still recapture it in my mind, even to the flowers in vases.

I think the media have a very odd attitude towards convents and convent girls. They like to highlight the difference between aspiration and reality which is a natural part of human existence, so you have, 'Convent Girl Gets Married For Fifth Time', or whatever it is. I suppose it is just natural to focus on some kind of contrast. As far as male attitudes are concerned, it probably stems from suspicion of a community of women and probably somewhere deep down from a reaction such as, if they have lived together for such a long time they must be desperate for ME – the man. It is quite entertaining!

I don't think you could say that a convent education makes you a good person. Clearly it doesn't, and we all end up good or bad, according to our own later life decisions. But what it should do is leave you with values that remain, no matter how life diverts you from your aspirations. The danger in the past I think was that it left you with a sense of guilt because you failed to live up to those aspirations, but as far as I can judge from what my daughter says, that is not at all part of the process now. That really has gone. The values that are there are, hopefully, a support, not a burden. That is what convents are now trying to leave you with. Whether that's a change in convents or a change in the Church, it's difficult to distinguish, because convents are not separate entities, they are a reflection of the church of which they form a part, and that has changed. I think education in a convent, more than in an ordinary school, is about 'the whole person'.

Mary Kenny

Mary Kenny was born in Ireland and attended the Loreto College, Stephen's Green, Dublin. She was a naughty schoolgirl and was expelled at sixteen. She has been a journalist for thirty years, publishing on both sides of the Irish Sea. Her book *Goodbye to Catholic Ireland* went into three editions in the US and her biography of William Joyce, 'Lord Haw-Haw' appeared in Autumn 2003. She lives between England and Ireland, is married to Richard West and is the mother of two adult sons.

'Little girls love the accessories of religion: the Holy Communion frocks, the petals and processions ... and pretty little holy pictures of St Maria Goretti exchanged with friends, with tender little sentiments on the back.'

Something that has dogged me all my life is that I have a real problem with authority. I cannot see or endure anybody making a statement without wanting to contradict it – the *esprit de contradiction*. In some ways, of course, it has served me well because in journalism it is often piquant to have another point of view, not to say simply what everybody else is saying. When I was a young woman, I was very feminist, very rebellious, wanting to kick over the traces all the time. Now I call myself post-feminist, as I am rather critical of much of feminism. Everybody now takes feminist claims for granted, but I want to question them – are maternal feelings just 'social conditioning' or are women 'naturally' as they are?

This urge to question came up a lot in my convent school and of course a convent is a place where you have three or four hundred girls, so you have to run it on organised lines. You *can't* have everyone questioning structures all the time. I was expelled when I was sixteen and what Mother Superior said to me when I was leaving was, 'If you have one bad apple in the barrel, it will corrupt all the others.'

I think I did have quite a strong personality and I probably did have a capacity for corruption; *now* I see it from the teachers' view, of course. It is quite true to say that if you have one difficult child in a class, this can disrupt everyone. I now think it deplorable that naughty children cannot be expelled from school nowadays! For me, it acted like a cold bath. I came away utterly humiliated, thinking – I've got to make it on my own now.

And it made me very determined to make my own way in the world and to make some sort of success of my life, though it did cut short my education. It is interesting that at the age of forty-six, here I am, going to university at last, as a mature student, and, God willing, when I am fifty, I shall at last have my university degree. Thirty years later, and it has taken me all of those thirty years to catch up with the average undergraduate. Leaving school at sixteen made me very chippy. I have an intellectual chip on my shoulder about being undereducated, and an overdeveloped awe for scholarship of any kind. Nevertheless, psychologically, it was probably right for me to leave school at the time – I had that convent girl's yearning for 'the world', anyhow.

In Ireland in the 1950s and early 60s people had a very different attitude to third level education than they have today. It was looked upon, then, as an enormous privilege to go to university, a privilege that only extremely clever, and largely comfortably off, 'swells' could benefit from. Only very, very exceptional youngsters could go to university from a poor or modest background. (My family were not working class, but there was a certain amount of lace-curtain genteel poverty.) I think there were only two scholarships per county for those who could not afford the fees, and you really had to be one of the two brainiest individuals in the county to win through. And even then, people's families had to be enlightened enough to allow them to go to college, depriving the family of another wage-earner for some years.

I think this is one of the areas in which feminism tends to decontextualise the lack of opportunity for women in former times. Girls did not have as many choices in their careers, but poor boys often had none at all. In some respect the Marxist interpretation of social history is more thoughtful than the feminist one: whole classes of people were discriminated against, including, for that matter, Catholics. People didn't think so much in terms of choices, anyhow, but of survival, and of duty. However, a determined and motivated person could always win through, I believe, because, as the Reverend Mother would put it, 'backbone shows'. Very Victorian, yet the Victorian emphasis on 'character' is no bad thing.

You know what they say about convent girls – 'bad girls, good women'; that is the tradition. They're bad when they escape from the convent because repression begets reaction. My sister, who was at a strict Dominican convent, says she still hasn't got over how nice life is *in contrast to* the restrictions of convent school. There is this notion that you escape from the cloister, and you become wild. I think a lot of convent girls did throw their bonnets over the windmill and lead rackety lives, once free – I certainly did, anyway. But then again, I recently went back to a reunion of old girls, and I was truly impressed by what nice, responsible, sensible and serious citizens most of them had become – flowering into the kind of women who are indeed the moral backbone of any society, organising, involved and dependable. I think when they get to middle age, convent girls often do turn into what the nuns wanted them to be.

But then again I returned to the school itself recently, and the atmosphere is totally changed. It is like any normal secular school now, in the sense that it has lost that extraordinary Dracula's-castle, cloistered feeling which I remember so well: the long polished corridors, the smell of bees-wax, the stone, spiral staircase where nuns would flit like bats into Mediaeval cells, and the strange odour of the nuns' garments – a sort of 'sergy smell'. Each nun had her own bell-ring, based on a clever system of coding through long and short bell-sounds, something which must have gone right back to the Middle Ages and the great monastic periods. Now they use electronic buzzers, just as, sadly, so many Irish churches now use electric candles instead of tallow or wax. Modernity spoils an atmosphere which evoked continuity.

I think as you grow older you begin to identify not only with your parents but with the older generation in general, and you start to forgive them their little faults because you see it all from their perspective now. There must have been nuns, in my schooldays, who had lots of personal problems with community life, which is as difficult and vexatious as marriage can be. St Thérèse of Lisieux said that she felt like throttling the sister in the bench behind her, for rattling her rosary beads incessantly. These are the little things that can drive you demented. Our nuns were probably having difficulties facing episodes like the change of life; and then, they were still living in seventeenth century habits, and subject to quite extraordinarily strict and often unreasonably petty rules. So they had their own worries, but I do genuinely believe that most of the time they acted in the best interest of the children they taught and cared for.

The tradition of convent schools does really go right back in history, and it can be claimed as a feminist tradition, to some extent: some of these battleaxe nuns in the Middle Ages were extraordinarily strong and commanding women. Nuns also did many secular jobs – they were, for example, quite often surgeons: as late as the fifteenth century the official surgeon at Longchamps was a nun, and she held the post for thirty years. Of course, many of the prioresses came from feudally powerful families, so there was frequently a dynastic dimension to their position. The Protestant Revolution, as it is now called, rather put a stop to convent life in Northern Europe, and if you read Luther on convents – he deplored them – you can see this distinct suspicion that nunneries are hotbeds of feminism which have got out of male control. Protestantism did have a very elevated view of marriage, and in consequence, thought every woman should be married. It is true that some convents were on the decadent side – with bejewelled nuns living worldly lives – but many others were centres of female learning, and of welfare for the poor.

However, you did have this resurgence of convents, particularly in the eighteenth and nineteenth centuries, both on the Continent and in the British Isles, as well as in the overseas English-speaking world. Irish women were particularly active in founding new orders which were socially and educationally vigorous: Mother Mary Aikenhead began the Irish Sisters of Charity, who to this day do such wonderful hospice work; Mother Mary Martin began the Medical Missionaries of Mary, an order of nuns who are both nurses and doctors and run hospitals all over the world. Mother

Catherine McAuley is particularly interesting – she founded the Order of Mercy in the 1830s, with the special aim to 'educate poor little girls, to maintain and lodge poor young ladies, and to visit the poor'. She felt particularly strongly that poor girls should have an education as good as their richer sisters, which was radical thinking indeed in the age when Catholic emancipation had only barely given male Catholics the vote.

You do, of course, have class differences with convent life – they're only human, after all. The Sacred Heart convents had the reputation of educating the daughters of gentlemen and ladies: they were very grand. The Loreto order, though broad enough in its intake, was touched with that old-fashioned we would now say pre-Thatcherite – snobbery. The worst possible fate they could envisage for one of their pupils was 'ending up working in a shop'. 'If you don't study, you'll end up behind Woolworth's counter!' they would cry. Nice girls didn't go into trade, you see. They made glancing references to their pupils as 'the mothers of tomorrow' but they were not at all heavy on marriage: getting a good job was presented as a much more important immediate aim. Indeed, there was an almost utilitarian obsession with passing exams and getting good marks.

At school, I was frequently in trouble because I was a very difficult and troublesome child. I think it would now be said that I needed an educational psychologist. I was one of those mixed-up brats; but I guess I did have background problems. I lost my father when I was very young, and I was the last, by a long shot, of a family of four. In some ways, I think I started out as an unwanted child, though as I grew older I became rather the apple of Mama's eye; one of the reasons, I think, why I am against abortion is that in my own life, I know, emotionally, that you can be both an unwanted pregnancy, and subsequently, an adored child. But being both neglected and then indulged is not good for the character, and I think now I was neurotic. One of my fellow-classmates was Brenda Fricker, the actress, and we were, I seem to remember, the naughty girls of the form. She had lost her mother quite young, and I have a feeling that the nuns wanted to be kind to her on that account. She was a sweet, angelic-looking young girl, but she was also seen as some sort of rebel or non-conformist. She was very popular; as a day-girl she would always do errands for the boarders.

I think in some ways it is sensually rewarding to be a Catholic when you are young. It is seductive, especially – yes, this is a sexist remark – for girls because little girls love the accessories of religion: the Holy Communion frocks, the petals and processions, the veils and holy water and lighting of candles and pretty little holy pictures of St Maria Goretti exchanged with friends, with tender little sentiments written on the back. I certainly know of Protestant little girls who were taken away from their adored convents because their parents grew very concerned about the passion with which girls throw themselves into Papist practices, and the extraordinary seduction of smells and bells. It seems to me that religion is also for enjoyment, however, and if smells and bells are satisfying to the spirit, why not?

My heart turns over now when on Corpus Christi the

BBC announcer proclaims 'Stock exchanges were closed today because it is a Bank Holiday on the Continent.' I think – *this is Corpus Christi*, a great Christian feast which all of Europe has celebrated for yonks! Do not reduce it to the banality of a holiday for a bank. In the secularisation of society, we have lost something of our heritage, those feasts and holy days that are so voluptuously celebrated by the great painters.

There is no doubt that the sensual side of convent life does stimulate the imagination, but there was also the tradition of the rational hammered home as well – Thomas Aquinas and the five conditions of the Just War, and all that: that we could perceive right and wrong also from our reason. Catholicism, of course, has fifty-seven varieties and you can usually find what you want in it. It is a mystical faith, on the one hand, but on the other, there is a tremendous appreciation of the body – there is indeed a worship of the body, if you look at the statues of Bernini and Michelangelo – those beautiful young men, those Madonnas in all the glory of the flesh. 'And the Word was made flesh': at the centre of it all is the *incarnation*. However, Catholicism can give contradictory messages in its appreciation of the body: there is the celebration of the body in every church painting, and yet there is the mortification of the body's desires both through martyrdom, and through chastity and celibacy. I think the nuns were ambivalent because while they talked a lot about chastity and modesty and shunning 'the occasion of sin', they unconsciously also portrayed sexuality as a garden of delights, something that God had made intensely pleasurable on purpose.

Biologically speaking, of course, they were speaking exactly; nature has indeed ensured the pleasures of sex deliberately, for her own interests.

They did have a very wary view of men, and here again, I am reminded of some feminist attitudes. The nuns regarded men as primitive, even barbarous creatures who Only Wanted One Thing and it was up to women to control these wilder masculine urges. When certain feminists today proclaim 'all men are rapists', are they not merely reiterating what nuns from a Victorian formation implied?

Obviously, Our Lady was a very important role, and some people have felt that this was rather awkward in that she represented the impossible as a role-model: both virgin and mother. But you also had this quite larger repertory of saints to choose from and identify with. Again, there was an entire battery of amazing female saints from, say, St Catherine of Siena, who was not only a doctor of the Church but made such gestures as drinking a cupful of leper's pus just to show that nothing daunted her, to, say, St Brigid of Ireland, who, being beautiful, asked God to make her ugly in order to repel her suitors, or St Joan of Arc who led an army to victory. At the very least, all this is excellent for the imagination, and I think it is why Catholicism tends to produce writers. My convent education was terribly deficient on maths and the sciences, but sensitive on things like the appreciation of art and music. This notion that a cultivated person looks at paintings and is at least musically literate, has stayed with me, and indeed, increased with the years. My taste is slightly lace-curtain in these matters, but at my age, I am allowed to admit to liking nineteenth century narrative painting about lost orphans, and corny operatic airs with tunes to them.

Of course, the most important thing that has stayed with me is the faith. Catholicism has remained vitally important and central to my life. I would feel absolutely lost without it.

Annie Nightingale

Annie Nightingale was born in west London and began her career as a BBC local radio journalist rising to become Britain's first female DJ. She broke the all male DJ code to join Radio 1, where she remains at the forefront of cutting edge music. In 1998 Annie was voted Woman of the Year and won a Lifetime Achievement Award from the music industry. In 1999 she published her autobiography *Wicked Speed* (Macmillan), which describes her memories of 'swinging London' and encounters with The Rolling Stones and The Beatles. She attended the St Catherine's Convent School in Twickenham from the age of five to eleven. She has a son and a daughter.

'I'll tell you what the convent did for me: I never ever need to feel completely alone, or feel total despair.'

I went to a convent because my parents thought that it was the only school in the area where you'd be taught to speak 'naicely' . . . it was for 'naice' girls. I wasn't a Catholic and my parents were 'sort of C. of E.', but not particularly devout at all. In fact, I don't think the academic standards were very high and I remember my father used to get very upset about references to Joan of Arc and the way the nuns pronounced Rouen as 'Rooenne'. He'd grown up in France and he'd say: 'It's *Rouen!*' But they were all Irish nuns and they spoke with a strong Irish accent.

St Catherine's Convent was the home of Alexander Pope, right on the Thames at Twickenham. It was quite an interesting place to be because every time the tide was high the playground would flood and we'd all be really excited. It also had a grotto under the road leading from the main school to the annexe. It was studded with rocks and we thought they were all precious stones, great big emeralds. I mean, it's absolute rubbish but you believe that when you're a kid and we used to try and kick bits off the walls.

Some of the nuns we loved and I can still remember their names. They were Sister Mary Denis and Sister Mary Theckler. They'd give you lovely, glowing reports which I'm sure I didn't deserve. Some of the others we were terrified of; they were real dragons. Apparently, when I was first taken there for an interview the headmistress said 'You don't like me do you?' and I said: 'No, I don't.' I mean, the honesty when you're that small! But they took me on anyway.

It's very romantic when you're young. I loved all that sort of theatre and dressing up. I used to do the Stations of the Cross and I loved Easter when they would drape all the statues of the Virgin Mary in purple. It's very, very attractive. I used to enjoy the lessons where you had to draw the priest's vestments and the chalice – and all that ritual. I used to collect holy pictures and rosaries; you want all the trappings. Maybe collecting holy pictures was a precursor to becoming a pop fan, you know, after holy pictures you become a fan of Jason Donovan or whoever.

My parents started to get very concerned. I remember there was this one picture of Jesus on the wall and one of the nuns said to me: 'Now, if you look at the picture He has his eyes open, but if you concentrate for long enough you will see His eyes open and close.' Well, of course you can easily hallucinate if you look at something for long enough; we were all convinced. I think my parents thought: What's going on here? They thought I was heading towards being a nun and they said I would have to leave. The nuns were very cross.

They say that convent girls are the ones that go off the rails later. I mean, I left when I was eleven and went to a girls' public day-school where I was considered very flighty. It was the sort of school where if you weren't Oxbridge material they really weren't interested in you. I was not considered particularly academic and I think they rather disapproved of me. When I left and I said I wanted to be a journalist; it was not considered the right thing to do. If you weren't going to university you were supposed to go to secretarial college or else you were not playing the game right. So I found one course in central London that did journalism and I said: 'Well, that's what I'm going to do.' And people said: 'Shouldn't you do a secretarial course to fall back on?' I said: 'I don't want to fall back.' I was obviously a rebel but whether it was as a result of the convent, it's hard to say.

I've often thought that it's not inconceivable that I would actually become a Catholic at some stage in my life. It's very attractive, it's very powerful, it's very beckoning. The long-term effect of my convent education is the guilt. I'm not a Catholic, but I've got the guilt. I just don't know why but it stays – it seems to stay with me forever. Sometimes I feel I've got all the disadvantages of Catholicism but not the advantages of it!

I was very, very friendly with a monk from the Benedictine Order at Worth Abbey. I even had my wedding reception there – it's a beautiful place and there was never that feeling of: Well if you're not a Catholic you're not coming here. Through him I met a lot of monks from other monasteries and they seem to have a very interesting attitude. They lead a very civilised, aesthetic existence. I can well see why people would be drawn to it. It's a hard life but they also know how to have a good time. My friend joined the Order late in life and before that he'd been an actor and a restaurateur and he'd led a pretty wild life. The monastery used to let him go to Paris for a weekend every now and then, just to let him have a bit of a fling because he obviously found the discipline a bit much. He was someone who had a tremendous effect on my life, who I knew I could always go and talk to and would be a good friend. Even though I was not a Catholic and I didn't live in the parish he was a lifelong friend.

Of course there's a lot of criticism of Catholicism. Well, it's all very fine that people who are terribly poor go to light candles when they can't afford to eat, and the church is so rich. But there's another side to it. I gatecrashed the Pope's Good Friday Mass in St Peter's, Rome, in 1989 and it was an incredible experience. There were nuns there from all over the world, there were people talking and chatting, and Japanese tourists standing on their chairs, taking photographs. It had more the atmosphere of a pop concert really.

Maybe there'll be a crisis in my life when I'll need something like that. Actually, I've got my own deal with God. I used to write for a teenage magazine and I wanted to address fairly serious topics but you have to do it in a fairly light-hearted way – otherwise young people think you're preaching at them. So I wrote this piece saying: How do you get in touch with God? Do you put an ad in *The Times* saying: Dear God, please call, phone or write? I had an amazing response from all these girls saying: Oh, we feel really sorry for you, we pray for you!

I find it really difficult to talk about this to anyone and it is really a personal experience that only happened to me but, about two or three weeks after that I felt I'd been 'contacted'. It was then that I felt I could just chat away and say: Well, I'm not asking you for this, but I'm very worried about so-and-so, please will you look after so-and-so. Sometimes

I'd do deals and say: If I do this, will you look after so-and-so. And sometimes I'd just say: Thanks mate. This is not getting down on your knees, it's all here, in the head. The trouble is, I find, when you ask God's advice, are you getting the answer you want to hear or is it just your alter ego? Only once have I ever gone against what He said. Or was that an inner voice? That's what bothers me. I'll never know.

If that's what the convent did for me, well . . . I'll tell you what it did for me: I never ever need to feel completely alone again, or feel total despair.

I remember the headmistress once saying: 'Fear knocked at the door, faith opened it and there was nobody there.' You know when you get a letter from the VAT or the tax man you think: I'm not going to open it, so you spend the whole weekend worrying about what's in it. And then you think, to hell with this and you open it and in fact it's not what you thought. That's quite a good thing to live by and it works.

Detta O'Cathain

Detta O'Cathain came into the public limelight in 1984 when she became a director of the Midland Bank, the first woman to join the board of any of the five big clearing banks. She followed this success by becoming Managing Director of the Milk Marketing Board and in 1989 was appointed to one of the most prestigious jobs in the arts, Managing Director of London's Barbican Centre. Since 1998 she has been President of the Chartered Institute of Marketing and in 1991 she became Baroness O'Cathain of The Barbican when she was appointed a Life Peer.

'They made the rules and I broke them. It's rather like parking on a double yellow line. You can't expect not to be clamped or towed away ... The rules were there and I knew about them from the time I was knee-high.'

The older one gets, the more relaxed one is about things. At the time I think I found my schools very restrictive. I was very much a freewheeler as a child. There was a gap of a year and nine months between me and my brother and he was the focus of attention. I was allowed to go off and do tomboyish things. I was fairly headstrong. The convent was my first experience of being corralled. At home I was really allowed to do what I wanted.

By the time I got to the second school in Limerick, I had adjusted to that and I found it much easier. It was just a process of growing up. I didn't feel unhappy, I felt I was being cared for and I was regarded as important. We were all regarded as important, not that I was more important than anybody else.

The academic standards were very high in both schools. My parents put great store by that. They said: 'We have no money, but what we will give you is the best possible education.' If the nuns were good teachers it was because they were single-minded. They didn't have to hurry off home to look after husbands and kids, they didn't have problems about mortgages, about organising the school car run. They were cocooned in their own convent and they could dedicate their whole lives to bringing up these girls and that's what they did.

A convent leaves you with a strong sensory experience. At the Loreto convent in Dublin we used to march and drill for deportment and poise. I remember we used to always line up outside the kitchens and I can remember the smell of stale cabbage. I can't stand cabbage. I don't think I've eaten it in forty years. Also, at Laurel Hill it was the bells. It was always bells. Bells in the chapels and bells in school at the end of break. I rather liked the bells actually, they were those old-fashioned kind of handbells. I remember the smell of incense in the church and the smell of roses in the May processions. And cheap perfume! That was the great thing, coming back to school after Christmas the dormitories used to reek of cheap perfume.

I found that the May processions were all right for the conformists but not very good for people like me who weren't conforming. They were spectacular and very beautiful. They used to crown the statue of Our Lady in the grounds and everyone wore white dresses with white veils. All the youngsters used to go beforehand and throw rose petals. The older I got the more I found this rather restrictive. I suppose it's the crocodile principle, going out for walks in crocodile and always looking alike. I got to the stage where I realised that human beings aren't all alike and they shouldn't be made to feel as though they are cloned. There was one serious occasion in my school life when I was in the fifth form, a very highly regarded member of the senior school. The girls were all singing Ave Maria and I started singing a pop song from the early 50s, 'Bimbo – Bimbo . . .', right past the Reverend Mother's study. Of course I did it to get peer group approval. Terrible really. I got severely told

off. It was quite a shocking thing for me. I wasn't quite
threatened with expulsion, but I was told my family would
be very upset. In fact my uncle was a Professor of Education
and he had trained many of these nuns, so they knew he
would not be pleased. I built up a great relationship with
him subsequently and although I never told him of that
incident I feel he would probably have been quite amused.

I think the nuns handled you rather well. They would let
you go to the limit of acceptable behaviour and once you
got over that you were told off, but you were always told
why. I was told that what I had done was an extremely bad
example to the seven- and eight-year-olds. It wasn't very
clever because I remember when I was a youngster looking
up to these fifteen- or sixteen-year-olds and thinking they
were gods – or goddesses. They were role models and at that
stage, I was a role model to them.

I had very strong set limits at home as well as at school. I
grew up during the 40s and early 50s when there were a lot
of constraints, a lot of restrictions. There were financial
constraints, there were consumer constraints, there were car
constraints. Not everybody had a car, there were lots of
things that you couldn't do. Somebody put this very well
when they said to me: 'Just because you like diamonds, you
can't rob a diamond mine.' I think that was the thing. It was
a case of, this is your area of operation; you are not the
daughter of the Queen of England, you can't just do that.

I think I probably did feel constrained and certainly looking back on it, when I first left school, I felt naive and very
unsophisticated. I was very ill at ease in my relationships
with the opposite sex and relationships with people in

general. You were cocooned for such a long time from the age of four to seventeen, and then suddenly you were thrown out into this great wide world, where nobody really cared whether you were bright or weren't bright; whether you had friends or whether you didn't. There you were. You had to take your place.

The outside world wasn't dwelt on at school and I think that's probably one of the negatives. It was painful, but I don't think it was any more painful than anyone else experiences in the process of growing up. I felt very conspicuous, I didn't feel I had any social graces. I felt I was suddenly thrown into somewhere where people really didn't necessarily like you. They used you or abused you. You weren't anyone special. Whereas when you were in school you were always special to some group. You were either special because you were good at a particular subject and you were a leader in your class, or you were a headgirl or a team prefect.

I'm a disciplinarian myself and I think a lot of my so-called perceived success has been due to the fact that I am very self-disciplined in terms of my work, in terms of setting objectives and trying to meet them. I think this was all instilled in me both at school and at home. I would be quite a different person if I were growing up now. And not, I think, as good a person. That sounds as if I think I'm a great person – I don't at all, but for me, for my character, self-discipline was essential. It is also essential in terms of my Christian beliefs. I do believe in the link between the word 'discipline' and 'disciple'. I think we are Christ's disciples and discipline is carrying out Christ's teachings . . . very badly in my case, but I try. I think that without that over-hanging rule, either spoken or unspoken, I would not have coped as well with life as I think I have coped.

Christianity is fundamental to my view of management, my particular management style. I do treat everybody as I would want to be treated. There are certain passages of scripture that I constantly relate back to and although some-times people would say I am ruthless, I always believe in doing what I think is right in terms of the greater good. Sometimes you have situations where you have to say to people: 'Look, we've come to the parting of the ways, because it is obvious that a) you're unhappy here or b) you're not making the contribution that is necessary, or, c) you're a disruptive influence.' I can always rationalise that back by saying, 'Look God gave us all talents in different directions, let us try to go through this together and see how I can help you find the right place for you to be rather than a square peg in a round hole.'

Discipline and creativity are natural adjuncts really. If you had unbridled creativity and you could do exactly as you liked, it could amount to anarchy. Whether we like it or not, the world is full of systems, economic systems, national systems, family units and you have to try and work out the best *modus vivendi*. To try and allow creativity to have its full flowering, you still need to put some constraints on it. You have to ask: is it commercial? If it is not commercial, how are we going to fund it? If it is not funded how is it going to continue? Because unfortunately everything comes back to money, everything we do. We can't carry on and just spend money as though it was going out of fashion. I think my colleagues here have enjoyed this approach. It's quite remarkable how some of these very creative people are now using their creativity to come up with suggestions on the commercial side. I suppose it's the same thought process as they use for creativity but now it is being channelled in some way to take account of commercial factors. The reverse is also true. Whereas I've always been regarded as a fairly cold, commercial animal, I'm now beginning to soften at the edges and become a little more creative and appreciate creativity a lot more. That's why this job is so wonderful because it has all the aspects necessary for making a real person.

I often take a black and white view because if you do that you can encourage debate and greater examination, analysis and consideration of a problem, provided you have good supportive staff around you who will say: 'Hold on Detta, it can't be that black or that white.' I sometimes play this game where I will take a very outrageous position just to see how they react. That's good psychologically, it's a good ploy.

My one problem with Catholicism is guilt. It's a major, major problem for me. It was only relatively recently at the age of fifty that I suddenly realised that religion is not supposed to be all hellfire and brimstone. I believed life was not fair, life was unhappy and you're not supposed to be joyful. But actually if you read Romans you suddenly realise that Christianity can be joyous. We should be really joyful that we have this wonderful gift from God, of being Christian. It's terribly late in my life to have discovered this. All the time I look back and I am horror-struck with some of the things that have been on my back for years as guilt. You just can't get rid of it. Even now, although I feel more relaxed about it I still have this overwhelming guilt. My friends keep saying: 'Detta, not again. For God's sake stop the guilt!'

Looking back on my childhood and my teenage years, I had a very negative approach to life, because the Christian ideal seemed so unattainable. I mean there was no question, as soon as you got up in the morning, you were guilty. There was something you didn't do correctly – you didn't fold your pyjamas the right way, you didn't put the water in the wash hand basin the right way. It was always negative and I began to look at things negatively and I've had to work very hard at that.

Now I'm the one who looks at things absolutely positively. Whenever some horror strikes or some trauma arises in the family, in the workplace, in relationships with people before I even open my mouth, I'll search through my mind for something positive. I'm known for being extremely positive and I think that has a direct relationship to the awful problems I had when I was growing up. That is a Catholic thing. I mean something naughty can actually be monumental in your own mind as a child. It can be like an adult committing murder, for a child to do something stupid like stealing somebody else's rubber or kicking somebody in the shins. You just get consumed with guilt and think well, all hope is abandoned, I might as well just go and do my own thing. People say: Well I don't want any of this any longer. I don't want to be disciplined, I want to be a freewheeler.

I was born a Catholic, baptised a Catholic and was very religious. Then I met and married my husband who had been married before. Because he was divorced the Catholic

Church said: Well you can come to Mass but you can't have any of the sacraments and that's it. I am the kind of person who could never be a part-time member of anything, it's the black-and-white thing again – you're either in or you're out. I thought well, to hell with that. At that stage, thirty years ago, there was no grey area in the Catholic Church. There was nobody there to say: Look we'll try and help you through this. Bill, my husband was quite prepared to convert to Roman Catholicism because he realised just how much my faith meant to me. I talked it through eventually with a Vicar who really encouraged me and now I'm a very committed, working member of the Church of England.

It doesn't really hurt now, after all I was the one who 'sinned'. They made the rules and I broke them. It's rather like parking on a double yellow line. You can't expect not to be clamped or towed away. I broke the rules. The rules were there and I knew about them from the time I was knee-high. I broke them and I really didn't expect an exception to be made. I don't criticise the Catholic Church at all.

What I would love to see is the Catholic Church moving towards the Protestant churches and vice versa. I live in Arundel in West Sussex where of course there's a strong local Catholic community with a Catholic cathedral. There's tremendous cross-fertilisation – strange to tell, an awful lot of people in our church are ex-Catholic – and we're all great friends. I think it would be wonderful if just one of the churches shut down and everybody went to the same services. Because in fact there's hardly any difference between them, in the words and even in the hymns they sing. So, I'm hopeful, although I think this problem of the ordination of women is going to be a setback. The Catholics are not going to accept that. I mean they're certainly not going to be able to accept it for the next hundred years. I think we've got to accept that. If there are givens, you don't fight against them. You hold back your ammunition to fight against something else where you have a chance of winning. I always say: Look I can't grow pineapples in the middle of London without some artificial aids, like heaters and green-houses, so what's the point. You've got to take things as given.

I don't think my marriage is wrong. I think probably God has forgiven me. I hope He has anyway. Two wrongs would-n't have made a right. I couldn't have copped out after a few years and said: Well, cheerio, I'm breaking up this marriage and going back to the Catholic Church. I mean that would have been a very great wrong. I think it has put a greater onus on me to make up for the wrong I did, by trying that much harder.

If there was one thing I got from my convent education it was humanity . . . to try and think of other people. I was very wayward and wilful as a child and it was self-self-self all the time and you would suddenly realise that it wasn't pos-sible. I went back to the school several years ago and I met one Sister who said she had been terrified of *me*. She said I was much brighter than the others and needed so much controlling. I was completely taken aback. I remember I used to be able to suss out who was bright and who wasn't amongst the teachers. There was one particular nun who used to parade up and down the dining room like a ship in full sail, keeping a beady eye on the tables. She would tell us to eat everything up and remember the starving children in Europe. She came past my table one day and I had a whole pile of salt on the side of the plate and she said remember the starving children and I said: 'Salt's not really going to be any use to them,' and she turned and went out. I was playing to the gallery and everyone thought it was hilariously funny. When I went back to the school for a reunion twenty-five years later I was told that in that instance she had gone outside and burst into tears. That made a lasting impression. It is a horrible thing to discover twenty-five years later. I'm sure I've done that unwittingly in my life a hundred times since then, but that was wittingly. I'd sussed out that she wasn't very bright. It taught me humanity; it has certainly made me a better person than I would have been otherwise.

Mary O'Malley

Mary O'Malley was born in 1941 to an Irish father and an English Lithuanian mother in Harrow, Middlesex. She attended the Convent of Jesus and Mary, Harlesden from 1952 to 1959. *Once a Catholic,* written in 1977 was her first full-length play for the theatre and became an instant West End hit. It won her huge acclaim, both from the critics and from the thousands of convent girls who had shared the experience.

> *'I feel uncomfortable every time I see a nun. I was doing a keep-fit class in a Catholic church hall one day when two nuns walked in. And I had a fleeting thought: Oh God I've got a leotard on, it's rude!'*

Actually it was a good school academically, and we had some teachers that weren't nuns, but from the religious point of view it was very frightening. I passed the 11+ to get there, thinking I was going to Enid Blyton territory, but it wasn't like that at all.

The nuns were mostly Irish, except for the headmistress who was frostily English. There was a kind of violence underneath the habit all the time, simmering away but never quite boiling over. Everything we did was wrong and you lived in fear of being found out. I was frightened all the time I was there but I put on a brave front. I used to wear my beret pulled down over my head just like a clown; I was always messing about but inside I was really scared all the time.

I think the fear was something to do with 'Our Lady'. We were expected to be like Our Lady, especially if you had a name like Mary, which fifty per cent of us did! Our Lady was looking at you all the time, spying at you from the clouds. She stood in the corner in statue form. She was another nun and you felt that wherever you went you were doing something wrong.

They didn't punish us physically. At home and at my primary school I was used to being hit, but they didn't do that. They specialised in psychological punishment which didn't seem as bad. I know it is bad, but to me at least I wasn't getting beaten, so I could stand any kind of mental punishment. You were humiliated all the time, out of the blue for something you didn't know you'd done. They would ask a question but wouldn't pick anyone who put up her hand. They'd pick on someone like me who didn't, couldn't answer the question and was made to look like an ignorant fool.

The uniform had to be just right. Everyone had to wear the same thing and you were supposed to wear long knickers, but we didn't unless we had games or PE. The fact was, I didn't mind that sort of thing. I liked the whole idea of going to a school in a uniform. It was the religious thing I didn't like. They would switch very quickly from being teachers to being nuns and you never knew when they were going to do it. I just wanted to be a Protestant really and go to a normal school.

Most of the nuns had come from Ireland, from the country, and had seen no life. I think Irish Catholicism is particularly bleak and martyred. I had all the same thing at home as well. There's great emphasis on martyrdom. I remember having an ulcer in my mouth and being told to put salt on it, and then, of course, to offer up the pain for all the souls in purgatory. Any kind of suffering had to be offered up for these bloody souls in purgatory. But who were they anyway? I couldn't get a picture of souls in purgatory at all.

There was no affection, no love of people at all. There was great love of God, of Our Lady and the Saints, but not people. They were superior because they had the gift of faith. I hadn't got that and therefore I wasn't worthy, I wasn't good. You could be good academically by working hard but you'd never be a good person. One nun said to me, when no one else was listening, 'You'll never be any good Mary O'Malley', after I'd committed a very minor offence.

As far as sex education was concerned there wasn't any. The word 'body' itself was a bad word. I went to this school at the age of eleven and I didn't understand why. Up until then I'd done a lot of dancing with my legs showing and suddenly we had to be sure that our shorts were no more than six inches above the knee. It was all very confusing. We had biology lessons which were all to do with rabbits. On our first day there, a little ten- or eleven-year-old girl put up her hand and asked how did parents know whether their baby was a boy or a girl. There was just a stunned silence from the nun who then said crossly: 'Your mother will tell you that.' The child obviously didn't know the first thing but we knew from then on not to ask any questions. It just left me with a sense of guilt. Guilt every time I see a nun, guilt in general. I was doing a keep-fit class once in a church hall and two nuns came in and I had a fleeting thought: Oh God, I've got a leotard on, it's rude! They thought the jiving we used to do in the 50s was immoral – I wonder what they'd think of the Lambada.

When I came to write *Once a Catholic*, I'd already been writing about Catholicism because that was what I knew most about. I was an expert in bigotry. That was what they taught us although at the time I didn't even know the word. The Catholic Church was all that mattered; anybody else could go to hell – or limbo – literally. I was just full of it. It was coming out of my ears, bigotry, bigotry, bigotry. That's what *Once a Catholic* is about.

It was commissioned for the Royal Court Studio Theatre Upstairs which was tiny. As I was writing it I thought: it would be nice if this could go on a big stage, but I never imagined how successful it would be. I didn't think it was that good as a play because I hadn't written that many. But it wasn't so much writing it, it was acting it. It's easier for me to be those nuns rather than actually write it down. I mean, I was those nuns and those girls while I was doing it. One of the Irish nuns, who had moments of reverting to a human being, and once confided to us in class that she used to smoke in the fields at home as a young girl, said to me one day in the garden where I was messing about: 'Mary O'Malley, you're a born actress.'

I was accused of having written an autobiographical play. One critic said: she has total recall of her schooldays, which I didn't. Much of the religious detail I had to get from a Catholic bookshop. But I wanted to relate to other people, I didn't want to just put my experience down, that's something you learn from drama. It wasn't about me, although I have been all those three girls in the play. I have been the little innocent when I first went there; then the hypocritical one and also the rebellious one who went out with boys. Most women will have been those three and many other characters. I felt intuitively that it wasn't just my experience but that it was everybody's who had been to a convent school. At the time of writing the play I now know that I had very few conscious memories of school or childhood. The memories came back to me later when talking to a

clinical psychologist after a road accident and two opera-
tions. Significantly I chose to be operated on in a hospital
run by nuns, and by a Catholic orthopaedic surgeon.

> The final scene of the play takes place in the school chapel
> where benediction is taking place. Mary McGinty, the
> naughtiest girl in the class, sticks a plasticine 'willy' onto the
> crucifix and runs off . . . It obviously caused a great furore
> amongst Catholics.

I think that scene was something very innocent. It wasn't to
do with a grown-up willy, it was a child's version of a willy
which is a long, thin bit of plasticine. Anyone who saw it as
a phallic symbol got it all wrong. The nuns, and indeed
everyone in the Catholic Church, have got this thing about
bodies and it drives me mad. That scene was a child saying:
'Look stop all this nonsense about bodies, I'm fed up with
it.' That's all it was to me. Saying to the Church, will you
leave our bodies alone please, because some of us don't
want to do rude things particularly and stop telling us all the
time that we're going to, or we're in danger of it! If I was
writing the play now, I think it would be more emotional
because I've been through a lot more. My children are
grown up and it all seems a long time ago. I was involved in
a car crash some years ago in which I was injured, not too
badly but badly enough to wonder whether it was a punishment for having written Catholic plays. I'm terribly grateful
now for being alive – and a bit more spiritual I think.

I don't feel bitter about my education. It's fun to look
back on it and it's good to meet other Catholics and laugh

about it. Even at the time, we laughed. We imitated the nuns and committed mortal sins and didn't die or go to hell. I don't think we were ever crushed by it, but I was frightened at school, of being humiliated and of being different. There were rumours that girls whose parents gave money to the school were better treated and I think that was true. I had one friend and we were so bad together that we had to be separated. We played truant, we wore our uniform in a slick way and we were a bad influence on the other girls. We were not allowed to join the Sodality of Our Lady because we were not worthy. We used to swagger round after school and talk to boys on street corners.

All through one's life, you're trying to shake it off, to come to terms with it. For me, the crunch came when I committed my first mortal sin. I didn't go to Mass . . . deliberately. We were told at school that the deliberate missing of Mass was a greater sin than to murder someone. So I waited for something to happen. Nothing did. I wasn't struck down, I wasn't punished. Having got away with it, of course, I went on to commit more mortal sins!

The guilt goes hand in hand with a convent education. In adult life you feel you're never good enough. That you don't deserve anything, that if something good happens to you, then something bad is going to happen to spoil it. You've got to suffer. Why? Because Our Lord suffered and all those saints suffered. If you go through the Book of Saints, it lists all the martyrs and the terrible ways they died for their faith. It's frightening to me, I can't cope with it. Why can't it be a joyful religion? It's always got to be suffering. Irish women in particular, nuns and mothers, revelled in suffering because it made them better Catholics. At the time I concentrated on the funny things. Children are very resilient, they shrug things off. It's later that it all came back to torment me, in quiet moments, in the middle of the night.

I am still a Catholic. In my own way. I don't like all the congregation business and all the social thing that it entails, gossiping and looking to see what people are wearing. But if I do feel the need for worship or prayer I like to go to a Catholic church on my own and light candles. I used to love the Latin sung mass. I don't like the mass now it's in English. I've never got used to it. I'd rather sing the *Credo* at home.

Anne Robinson

Anne Robinson was born in Liverpool and attended convent schools for all of her school life, spending the final years at the Farnborough Hill Convent boarding school in Hampshire. Anne left school at 16 and embarked on a career in newspapers and broadcasting. She wrote a personal column for several national newspapers and was the first woman to regularly edit a Fleet Street paper. She presented her own interview show on BBC Radio 2 and her television work included *Points of View* and the consumer programme *Watchdog* for BBC 1.

More recently she achieved international success with *The Weakest Link* game show, broadcast in both the UK and the US. Anne has published an autobiography, *Memoirs of an Unfit Mother*, and was appointed Honorary Fellow of Liverpool John Moores University in 1996. She has married twice and has a daughter, Emma, born in 1970, who works in television and radio in New York.

'If you have ever stood on a chair with your green knickers showing in front of 200 girls, reading out loud from a holy book – nothing truly daunts you after that.'

I always wanted to go to boarding school. I had always been at a convent school but I had read a lot of Angela Brazil and the Twins at Mallory Towers – or were they St Clares? Anyway, I just thought it would be very exciting to go to a convent boarding school. In fact, it didn't really live up to my expectations although it was still exciting to be away from home and on my own. I had a brother who had gone to boarding school, so it seemed to me that I should be doing exactly the same.

I learnt very little during my time there in terms of academic achievement. I really didn't do anything. I got a few 'O' levels; but what I really learned a great deal about was survival and bucking the system, about being devious and never giving up. There was always a way round everything because convent life was made up, for the large part, of a lot of inexplicable, petty rules. They seemed to me to be petty rules, so you had to decide how best you could stay there with credibility but not do what they wanted you to do.

One of the particularly petty rules was that the new headmistress decided that all post must be opened unless it was from our parents. This was tricky because I had fallen deeply in love with a boy at my brother's school, Ampleforth. The highlight of term time was that he wrote to me. It was all very innocent but I was blowed if I wanted

Mother Rosemary Alexander to have a look at his letters first. I asked my parents to address twenty or thirty envelopes to me at the beginning of term and then I gave them to him. That way none of his post was opened on its way to me. Now that was a prime example of how they got you into a bit of lateral thinking. Mind you, you need liberal parents!

If we were ever doing anything important, the nuns told us to sit up straight and put our shoulders back. It was absolutely vital that you curtsied to visitors and to the Reverend Mother. It was particularly tricky because there was this glass parlour and if you walked past it when there were visitors in, and you were on your way to the library with a pile of books, you had to curtsy sideways. We became very good at it.

Last year I met Prince Edward and I was told beforehand that I only had to shake hands with him. But when I got up to him I said, 'I hope you don't mind, Sir, but I am actually going to curtsy because it cost my parents about ten thousand pounds for me to get the hang of it, and I would like to be able to ring my father up and finally tell him, thirty years later, it's all been worthwhile.'

They did give you this idea at Farnborough Hill that you were someone rather special. Now that isn't elitist because I think that women desperately suffer from lack of self-esteem. I think to have left school with a bit of a feeling that I was somebody special wasn't bad. They did like you to consider yourself a cut above the others. A cut above the world.

It's only looking back that I realise that quite a lot of

emphasis was placed on who had money at school. I'm not sure that is particular to convents, I wonder if it isn't just something that happens at boarding schools. There was a flip side to that coin though. Recently I met someone who was a generation ahead of me at Farnborough. She had come as a girl from Poland, her parents had moved over here and halfway through her education they had gone back to Poland only to find that they could not get out again. So there she was at Farnborough Hill with no relatives in this country and the nuns kept her. Obviously no fees were paid and they kept her there during the holidays as well and looked after her. She went on to medical school and became a doctor.

We had no sex education at all. We would have all gone to our graves as virgins if it had been left to them. In my fourth year I discovered there was a book in the library called *Growing Up*, or so it was whispered. It took ages and ages of putting your name down on a very, very long waiting list to get this dog-eared copy of it which eventually explained the sexual act to me for the first time. But that was the late 50s, early 60s. It's very different now.

There was also a lot of emphasis on sin and a lot of talk about 'big sin', and how it was sinful to be 'bold'. 'Bold' was a word the nuns were fond of. 'Anne Robinson you're the boldest girl in the class.' The trouble was that as you got older it was really hard to try and believe what they were saying to you because so much of it seemed picky and petty. Also the nuns, mistakenly, did tend to punish you with church and punish you with chapel and punish you with mass. If you were late for Sunday Mass which was at eight o'clock you weren't allowed in. Instead you had to go to the High Mass in Farnborough itself, at the abbey in the town. I discovered that this was a really good idea because you could get out and have a good breakfast with one of the day girls, so they stopped that eventually. This was the way you found things out, you made the system work for you in the end.

I never went through a religious period. I prayed quite often for it to be the end of term but that was it. I spent a lot of time being locked up because I was opinionated at school and I was always talking too much. I don't know if I would have been opinionated anyway. I don't know if boarding school makes you resilient. I remember the very first time I read autocue on television. I was quite brilliant at it – and I knew exactly why. We used to have retreats at school which meant two whole days of absolute silence, two days of not speaking unless you absolutely had to. The headmistress knew full well that this was quite impossible for me, so she decided on a policy of damage limitation which was to have me doing something which would stop me disrupting the rest of the school. She made me stand on a chair at the corner of the refectory and read out loud to the whole school at meal times. I do think that if you have ever stood on a chair in front of 200 girls with your green knickers showing, reading out loud from a holy book, nothing truly daunts you again.

Catholicism is not a religion, it's a nationality. I think that we are always, always Catholics. Mother Alexander wouldn't think I was a Catholic, but I know I'm a Catholic. If I bang my toe, I will suddenly say 'Jesus, Mary and Joseph'! I never went through a period of thinking that it was something I should dismiss. I never really went through a rebellion with Catholicism. I began to believe that I was perfectly within my right to make up my own definition of Catholicism. I think now I'm best described as, I hope I am, a Christian. I am certainly someone who prays. I get exasperated with the changing rules of the Catholic Church because there are a lot of things that were totally out of order when I was young that are now positively encouraged. For example, when I was very young, five, I remember going along with a friend of mine who was a non-Catholic to her church one afternoon. We had nothing better to do, just to have a look round at the church at the top of the road. I was still at kindergarten then and on Monday morning I was telling Mother Regina what I did. Well, goodness me, my parents were called in to the school and asked what was I doing in a non-Catholic church. Well, nowadays, every effort is made to get us all together, so that leaves you without any respect for some of the rules. So I don't see any need to do exactly what the Catholic Church says, but it has left me with a sense of God and a sense of religion. I firmly believe in miracles!

John Walsh

Journalist and broadcaster John Walsh is the son of an Irish doctor and an Irish nursing sister. He was born and brought up in South London, educated first by the Ursulines, then the Jesuits, and attended the universities of Oxford and Dublin. He is the Assistant Editor of *The Independent* and author of *Growing Up Catholic*. His book of memoirs *Are You Looking At Me? A life through the movies* is published by HarperCollins.

I was actually a 'convent *schoolgirl*' for a year by an odd mistake. I grew up in Battersea and my parents found that the best Catholic school in the vicinity was the Ursuline Convent in Wimbledon, six miles away. There was a sense that a Catholic education was intrinsically better than a non-Catholic one, the way they taught you everything, from English to Maths would naturally be better as well as the teaching of right and wrong, religion and morality. My sister went there too, in the class above me.

I started there when I was four and was still there when I was eight. In the third year, all my little chums, the boys in their short trousers, went off to the Jesuit prep school in the next street, but because my birthday fell at the end of the year, I just missed the closing date so I had to stay in the first form, the only boy in a class of twenty-four girls. I was an honorary convent girl which is why I have become a repressed nymphomaniac! I wasn't conscious of any especial difference in the way I was treated, except that it was generally assumed by the teacher that I would necessarily be in some way naughtier.

I can remember in some lessons, I would act as the priest and all the little girls would be handmaidens around me. When you are seven this is very potent stuff.

When I was thirteen I decided I was going to be a Jesuit

and I remember telling my mother as she was closing the curtains in the living room and she stopped half way. There are some people, you can tell when they are moved, just from the back of their heads, you could tell she had huge tears in her eyes. She said, how *pleased*, and how *happy* I had made her by what I'd said. Then I told my old man who was a bit of a lad, to be perfectly honest, and he said: 'Hmm, how old are you? Thirteen, yes; well if you still want to be a priest in another year's time you're no son of mine ...' Unfortunately he was right; the usual demands of puberty took over, and rather put you off the vows of poverty and chastity.

What appealed to me was the *theatricality* of the Church. It comes into its own at Christmas and Easter, but every week there were a certain number of theatrical frissons available to you if you did the Stations of the Cross. You shuffled along with this curious little touristic gaggle around a series of fairly revolting icons – The Stripping of Christ and The Scourging, and The Crowning of Thorns and The Crucifixion. While the priest's voice rose to a pinnacle of disgust about 'those barbarians who flayed Him alive ... who nailed Him to a cross ...' it is curious, your heart would pound slightly faster, and you would feel rather over-whelmed. Naturally, in the way of teenage self-projection, you were putting yourself into it as well – *you* were being that hero that would somehow 'spring' Christ, and help him escape – although, of course, disappointingly, he never did.

There were all kinds of curious things you could never quite work out, such as: what exactly *was* on the altar?

There was a tabernacle with a little curtain in front of it and then a big heavy door, like the miniature doorway into the tiny garden in *Alice in Wonderland*. Occasionally they would open the door and you still couldn't see what was in it but you *knew* that there was something really exciting in there. At some point there would be what was called the Exposition of the Blessed Sacrament which lasted for three days. This was riveting because you were for the first time being brought face to face with the thing itself, the closest you would get to a reified God. In fact, all it was was a very large wafer that had been transubstantiated during Communion, a wafer transformed into the Body of Christ, the central mystery of the Mass. It would sit there in this spectacular glowing thing, like a vase but with great sharp spikes poking out of it. A priest would gather it up with incredible holiness into hands that were covered in great brocade robes. The priest would proceed up and down the aisle, surrounded by incense and crosses and as it went by, you were supposed to bow your head in reverence. But of course you couldn't because you were dying to see it close-up, just to investigate. It was always rather a disappointment that all you could see was a large round circlet of bread. I always fancied I could see something else in there, like a tiny attendant angel.

I was an altar server in those days, having to ring bells, having to wave a thurible at the 'audience' or congregation – again that theatrical image. After the Offertory you would turn round, and go to the edge of the altar steps, bowing at the congregation. Naturally you didn't think of yourself as a mere worker in the fields of the Lord, you thought you were Mick Jagger about to perform 'You Can't Always Get What You Want'. You would bow contemptuously at the congregation – all of whom immediately stood up. You waved the thurible of incense at them, bowed snootily again and wandered off – it was *terribly* theatrical. It left you feeling so in charge – such a *star*.

Things pursued you everywhere. If you got up in the night to have a glass of water, you would encounter a picture of the Sacred Heart of Jesus on the wall outside my parents' bedroom with a red light burning forever in front of it. I would hurry past this unlikely icon because I couldn't work out what it was for. It was like some bad taste advert for open-heart surgery – your Saviour holding his heart out to you. The heart was an extraordinary kind of cardiac strawberry which had beams of light radiating from it, like the advert for Pearl and Dean in the cinema. I stood there and looked at it in complete bafflement, not knowing why this uprooted organ was being presented for inspection. There was the face of Christ, with his long hippy hair and his beard, looking terribly sad – you just felt disconcerted more than anything else.

I think it is an extremely important and necessary part of education to teach children that there is such a thing as goodness and badness, rightness and wrongness. On the other hand if you persuade them that the most appalling torments imaginable will come and visit because they do something slightly wrong, I think that is an appalling thing. Teaching morality is fine if it is a contained morality; if it is backed up by these dreadful threats I think it is absolutely sickening and pernicious.

The fear of hell was far more potent than any expectation of heaven. Everything you did, everything you *didn't* do, they got you in every possible way, until you were likely to find yourself in this curious downward spiral where the chance of going to heaven seemed extraordinarily remote. You had to watch every single thing you did. If you failed to keep an eye out for people who were cold, hungry, naked, if you somehow neglected some duty which you only barely understood – that itself was a sin. If you were in a situation where to stay around could possibly lead to you committing a sin, *that* was already a sin. It was more a stick than a carrot. You were encouraged to exercise a constant internal vigilance like a sort of metal detector, to find out when you were doing something wrong, something inside you that would go 'bleep' and you would think, 'Ooh, no, I've done it again.' That is the way they got you: constant self-accusation, constant self-prosecution.

Catholic girls were a complete mystery. You were told at school about the sixth and ninth commandments: Thou Shalt Not Commit Adultery and Thou Shalt Not Covet Thy Neighbour's Wife – but somehow these would be extrapolated to mean that you couldn't indulge in whatever kind of strange fumblings and feelings that accompanied growing up. As a result, you got the impression that the girls *must* be almost equally to blame as yourself. The teachers kept trying to tell you that you would be subject to all kind of animal desires which would somehow meet an animal desire coming the other way. We would look at these little bundles from the convent, in their little cloche hats, their sensible purple uniforms and ridiculous blue socks, watch them prowling around the Downs – home of the Ursuline Convent in Wimbledon – and you just couldn't imagine that these ludicrous little parcels could have any kind of sexual presence at all.

In the sixties the word 'sin' was Fleet Street's euphemism for sex. The *News of the World* and the *People* would always talk about the 'City of Sin', sinful nightclubs and so on, so we confused in our mind the idea of wrongdoing in a religious sense exclusively with the idea of sex. The two deliciously collided when you saw Dusty Springfield, her incredible eyes drenched with make-up. She seemed so *naughty*, it wasn't true. She would talk about 'snogging in the back row of the cinema' which was considered an absolutely unspeakable subject. The same went for Marianne Faithful. She was a combination of doc-faced beauty with intense, experienced sexuality, like a kind of Bambi with a migraine, her blonde hair and these beautiful eyes and a vague notion she was terribly, terribly 'on for it' as the phrase went at the time. She seemed just very innocent and devastatingly sexy, a combination that was irresistible – something that you couldn't really relate to the girls that you saw around you. We would look at the girls in the next street and try and relate the image of the convent girl to the astonishing image of the wondrous Dusty. And Kathy Kirby, and the other icons of our day, with their amazing bosoms and their louche hair styles. We couldn't make any connection, because what we didn't realise at the time was that convent schoolgirls were undergoing such a fantastic process of repression. They would only become

like the Dustys and the Kathys four or five years later, and
when they did it was like a tidal wave.

My sister's pubescent friends formed a group called The
Fabs. There were about eleven or twelve of them and they
operated like a sorority, such as you'd find in Mary
McCarthy's book *The Group*. They tentatively investigated
things and wondered about boys and men; they'd pass on
little notes and write each other impassioned letters. By the
time one got to go out with them, they had an affectation of
certainty and sophistication which was never really quite
true, but which made you shake in your socks. It was as if
they'd never really been virgins at all, although they almost
invariably were.

In my sister's case, the first night she went out on a proper
date with a boy she was fourteen and a half. I was thirteen,
an innocent stripling. My parents, who were kindly and concerned, were sitting in the living room waiting for her to
come home, when my mother said to my father: 'Now look,
when she comes in, it will be a very difficult moment for her,
so for God's sake don't ask any awkward questions. Let her
tell us in her own words, in her own good time when she is
ready. She will be a bit scared, you know . . . worried . . . but
take it easy.'

So we sat there and I was thinking what is this? What will
she have been doing? It was riveting. At 11:30 on the dot she
came in, strode into the living room and flung her coat over
the side of the sofa and said, 'God, he's so inexperienced!'

It was a wonderful moment. She was fourteen and a half
and she did not know *diddly*, about anything – which made
such an affectation all the more spectacular.

Sin was an enormous and baffling subject because it seemed to encompass so many different kinds of activity. Basically it was divided into two kinds: mortal sins, which destroyed the soul or made it a huge great rotting excrescence, black and useless; it meant, if you died before you had gone to confession then you would go straight to hell, no mucking about, no appeal court.

Venial sins were milder forms, a momentary turning away from God. Venial sins were things like swearing. If you stole a very small amount of money out of somebody's pocket, just to be wicked, that was perhaps venial, although you had to watch it; if it went over five quid it was getting on to being mortal and you were in dead trouble – you had to watch the inflation rate to see if the line changed. Along the way there were some other rather puzzling things: to find that starting an unjust war or invading a neutral country, or even conducting an armed robbery was just the same as having very impure thoughts about Miss Springfield seemed unfair. That they would all send you to hell at precisely the same speed seemed very unfair indeed.

There were also, of course, the sub-venial sins, the Old Lady sins, as they were known. These were the ones my mother and her good Catholic lady friends would confess which weren't really anything – having vaguely erotic thoughts about Robin Day or somebody: being mildly irritated because a car runs over your foot.

Father Colliston, who took us for religious studies was extraordinary. He was quite keen on Six and Nine, as he always referred to them, the commandments Thou Shalt Not Commit Adultery and Thou Shalt Not Covet Thy

Neighbour's Wife. The first is broadened out to encompass all forms of sexual activity; the second one, about coveting is more about longing and gratified desire, about masturbation, about looking at 'immoral literature' and so on. What this priest would explain to us was what we *couldn't* do with a girl. It was the classic David Lodge thing of *How Far Can You Go?* It started with holding hands and kissing, with petting, with something called *heavy petting*, with something more disgusting called 'handling' and something which was actually intercourse, but it was never actually said. The baffling bit was about petting and *handling* – it took ages to work out what this actually meant. It sounded like handling stolen goods, or perhaps something to do with heavy machinery. Or something strenuously physical, like the manipulations of a chiropractor. In fact it meant masturbation. Gradually this became clear but very, very gradually. Any convent girl with any kind of decency at all would naturally have stopped you getting anywhere near halfway through this list. Well *yes*, we thought, but what about the *others*?

One would regret it, one would feel that something had been lost if Catholicism became like any other religion (when did you last hear of a lapsed Protestant?). But you cannot be nostalgic about these things. I have a daughter of three and the idea of sending her to a convent where she would endure the same things as my sister put up with is absurd. If the old repressions and superstitions were long gone one would welcome it because Catholicism is a tremendously positive religion. It tells you how the world is – of course it makes it all up a lot of the time. But it gives you a world picture, a home and a circle to live in which is tremendously reassuring.

But really what a Catholic education gives you is something to fight against. It doesn't set out to, of course, but it gives you something whereby you will have to become a hero unto yourself, or else cave in and become your parents' good little boy or girl. Confronting it makes you a fighter.

The best thing about being brought up a Catholic is that, after the incessant flood of negative things that are told you, the threats that are put your way if you allow one grain of ego to appear, it will probably appear earlier than in your non-Catholic counterparts – and it will be stronger, and last longer. You have to fight and I think in doing so one grows into a real person.

As for guilt, it became so natural it was almost like breathing after a while. If you meet another Catholic this word always comes up. It means that in your grown-up relationships with other people you are handicapped to an extraordinary degree. Your impressions of sex or sexual engagement are always hedged around by fright or worry or a feeling that something nasty is in progress. One loses that sooner or later, I'm happy to say, but in the early formative stages every Catholic is afflicted with it. There is a sinister side, certainly, the feeling that your body and your will are not your own, that you are not *doing enough* at all times, means that for the rest of your life you will always be at the mercy of this feeling of inadequacy, that it is *your fault*. You feel that with your husband, your wife, your mistress, the man who comes to read the meter, your boss at work, the Inland Revenue, it is always your fault. You will not argue,

but of course you may compensate for that by becoming a
sort of noisy bully. But it is a handicap that affects people
badly and it affects every Catholic, I think, for some time, a
central, disabling, cowed and craven sense that you're not in
charge of your own destiny.

Marina Warner

Marina Warner was born in London in 1946 to an Italian mother and English father. From the age of nine to seventeen she was a boarder at St Mary's, Ascot run by the nuns of the Institute of the Blessed Virgin Mary. As a writer, in studies of the Virgin Mary and of fairy tales, she has explored myths and symbols. She recently published *The Leto Bundle*, a novel, and *Fantastic Metamorphoses, Other Worlds*, based on the Clarendon Lectures 2001, given in Oxford. She lives in London.

'If you look at the history of Catholic thinking, this emphasis on the tremendous sinfulness of the flesh can be laid at Augustine's door. It is one of the tragedies of history that Augustine prevailed to the extent that he did.'

We'd been living in Egypt, where my Father was a book-seller and we found this enclave in west London near where we rented a flat. I think it shows the strength of the inter-national Catholic community that although my mother was Italian and we'd been abroad for some time I could imme-diately be instructed for my First Communion.

First Communion is probably the most important cere-mony for a growing Catholic girl. The imagery's really brought to bear personally for the first time – you're dressed as a kind of bride which suddenly plunges you into a world of such strong affections, such strong feelings and you feel you're very special. Catholics aren't allowed to have the body of Christ in the consecrated bread until they've a sufficient knowledge of the religion and its tenets. You have to learn the basic facts of the faith and it's only when you know them pretty much by heart from the catechism that you're then allowed to have your First Holy Communion. When you're baptised you're not 'conscious', so only at your First Holy Communion do you become a fully-fledged Christian.

I had a nanny who was an Irish Protestant, and just as I was going out of the door all dressed in my white robes she said to me, 'Lord! You haven't had any breakfast!' So she sat me down and gave me some biscuits just to be quick about it. My mother came in and said: 'But you're *eating*. You're not meant to be eating!' This was in the 1950s when you fasted before communion for virtually twenty-four hours, or certainly the whole night before. My mother was then faced with this awful decision of letting me continue or calling the whole thing off, because I was now in a state of sin.

In fact, I made my First Communion but it always did stick in my memory as a very bad beginning. I'm afraid that it stigmatised me, probably for life.

When I went to St Mary's Ascot, it seemed enormous and curiously impenetrable. I think in my mind it got mixed up with fairy tales because you went in through this slightly shaggy, overgrown country. There were very deep, dark, rhododendron bushes with lots of shadows and insects. When it rained they would drip and shine in the rain. Beyond that there was this tall pinnacled, Gothic, almost fairy-tale-like building where I was enclosed for what seemed like a very long time. My parents were living abroad again so I didn't even see them as often as other girls saw theirs. But even for the ones who had regular visits it was only three times a term in those days and there was no going home at half-term. It was very much the old-fashioned kind of boarding school, and set a very deep stamp on anyone who went there. It was our world. It was the place I spent most of my life in those days.

Invocations to the Virgin Mary marked out the days of my childhood in bells: her feast days gave a rhythm to the year. On the feast of the Purification we wore starched white veils of tulle that stood around us like a nimbus. With the medals of the Sodality of Our Lady on blue ribbons round our necks, we processed with lit candles up to the communion rails to be blessed.

The blue ribbons – blue is the colour of the Virgin 'the sapphire', as Dante wrote, who turns all of heaven blue – signified that the wearer was a child of Mary, and had dedicated herself to the Virgin and promised to emulate her in thought, word and deed: her chastity, her humility, her gentleness. She was the culmination of womanhood. As my agnostic father maintained, it was a good religion for a girl.

From *Alone of All Her Sex: The Myth and the Cult of the Virgin Mary*

It was a rhythmic life – we had a very organised day. We wore veils to go to Mass first thing and we went to Communion every morning. The day followed this rather monastic kind of rhythm. When you study the life of the monasteries in the Middle Ages it's very like the kind of life we led. I think this is why the church occupies you and takes possession in a very secretive way. You then have to fight against it, perhaps more violently than you would wish, because it has sunk so deep.

I was very docile as a child although I think I was turbulent within. I feel cursed, and this is actually shared by quite a lot of girls with my upbringing – we have a desperate desire to please. There's something maiming inside about feeling that if you're not actually pleasing the adult with whom you are talking, you're transgressing very deeply against the way you should be. The idea of obedience, of pliancy was the message of the Virgin Mary; we were taught that her first words had been: 'Be it done unto me according to Thy word.' I wanted terribly to be good and I think that this set up a kind of war within me that still goes on, between wanting to find a path to something I felt was true, but at the same time wanting desperately to please. I still have it strongly and often if someone says something I don't agree with I don't speak up because I feel it's a transgression. This was actually not just Catholic morality, this was Catholic morality for *girls*. The boys were trained to have a mind of their own and the idea of individual conscience was stronger for boys.

It's rather interesting that Mary Ward, who was the founder of the Institute of the Blessed Virgin Mary, had actually wanted in the seventeenth century to start an order of Jesuitesses. She said if boys are going to be taught to use their minds and be the intellectual soldiers of Christ, then I want young women to have the same chance. She began schools and ran into trouble with the clergy and was actually imprisoned at one time. Her convents were closed and she struggled throughout her life to establish the Order. Now, we were very much brought up with Mary Ward as our great foundress, but her story was not told exactly like that. There was something much more simple about the Mary Ward we were told about. She was not really this kind of struggler for women's rights at all, she was much more an exemplary self-sacrificial figure.

St Mary's was of course my first experience of an entirely female community. I owe the nuns an immense amount because they provided me with so much of my subject matter, I really have to be grateful to them. Without them I'd have almost no material and my imagination would be filled with very different things. They themselves were quite capable of rebelling and that's one of the paradoxes. While they taught you to be docile and silent they were independent and autonomous. This was the rather delicious paradox: the nun teaches her charges that women should keep silent in the church; as St Paul said, a woman should not raise her voice or assert herself, yet the nun facing a classroom of thirty or forty children is doing precisely that – asserting herself. The interesting thing is that the history of nuns often shows that the vocation attracted women of extraordinary spirit. It was one of the few ways that a woman who wanted to be a nurse or wanted to receive an education actually could do these things and this holds true since the Middle Ages. Many of the saints' lives tell about women who were reluctant to marry. They may have wanted to be chaste, but it was also because outside marriage they had a chance in convents for education and to do things other than keep a house.

I think in a practical way, single sex education is very good for girls. Sociological studies actually show that boys flourish in the company of girls because it makes them wish to excel, whilst boys tend to distract girls from their studies. The presence also lowers their own ambitions because they don't wish to outstrip men, which is a great misfortune. So, educationally the convent was rather an inspiring place with a richness of stories and good music. We had a Reverend Mother who actually composed her own masses and I used to sing in the choir; it was all very enriching. I owe the nuns a great deal as individuals as well. They very often bent the rules for me. I suppose the excitement of being Catholic is that you know where the boundaries are, but in a way that gives you an ability to break them. I was very interested in Latin and this interest was very much fostered by my Latin teacher. We had a locked cupboard in the library where books were kept because of their erotic subject matter. I wanted to read the Latin poets like Catullus and Propertius and she opened the cupboard for me.

> The world of music, flowers, perfumes and painting that enfold her (Mary) was filled with joy. It was only in the last two years at school, that I felt the first chill wind sigh in this blissful pleasure dome. Doubts about doctrine caused minor tremors compared to the absolute misery that shook me when I was confronted, in puberty, by the Church's moral teaching.
>
> The price the Virgin demanded was purity. Impurity, we were taught, follows from many sins, but all are secondary to the principal impulse of the devil in the soul – lust.
>
> From *Alone of All Her Sex*

Our curiosity about men was pure fantasy as the only men we ever saw were a few gardeners and herdsmen who were kept very far away from us. We still speculated about them of course and about the monks who came to say Mass. The image of the sexy convent girl is, I think, an example of a self-fulfilling prophecy. The more you hold up the threat and terror of what might happen, the more it tends to come true. There's a lot of comic jokes that arise out of people's prurience about nuns, and an almost seaside postcard mentality about nuns and convent girls, but I think convents themselves are colluding with this myth. When I was young there was such an extreme emphasis on the dangers of sexuality that it did actually put sex on the brain quite badly for us. It was all shrouded in secrecy so one was never quite sure what this sin was.

I remember my first picture book of the ten commandments. I knew that the picture for Thou Shalt Not Commit Adultery had something to do with sex, but the picture showed two children tearing up books and throwing them into a dustbin. I didn't actually make the connection for a long time that these books were dirty books and I suppose the problem is that you can hardly show a man kissing a woman who is not his wife! The problem of representation arose because of the problem of actual silence around the question.

We knew that Mary was perfect because of the virgin conception of Christ, that she hadn't had to do the thing that we didn't know what in order to have Jesus and I think that dismayed us. There's such a concentration on the theme of sex in connection with convent girls because it's an area fraught with all the moral questions of how to be a good person.

I was brought up at the absolute saturation point of a very old-fashioned kind of Catholicism in the fifties and early sixties. If you look at the history of Catholic thinking, this emphasis on the tremendous sinfulness of the flesh can be laid at Augustine's door. It is one of the tragedies of history that Augustine prevailed to the extent that he did. It was a time when people were thinking about the evil in the world and how it could be that mankind had in some way fallen. Many theories were produced but Augustine's prevailed. To put it crudely, Augustine's was that the root of all

evil was concupiscence and that woman was the inspira-
tion of this concupiscence. Like Eve, woman moves man to
sin, and so we, as little children and then as teenagers were
identified with this problem. Mary was exempt from it; she
had been spared it, but the rest of us had to face the fact
that we were blameworthy even without doing anything.
The great horror of it is that the analogy would be that the
rape victim is to blame for the rape. We were taught to consider ourselves blameworthy because women were sexual
creatures and if you think of yourself as a sexual creature
you tend to exude it. That's why convent girls are sexy
because they are constantly being admonished not to be
and they therefore become aware of themselves as carnal.

One of the people who opposed St Augustine was a man
called Julian of Eclanum who came from southern Italy.
He believed that sex was part of the human condition and
therefore had been instituted by God in some way and there
were very many greater problems of evil that we should
look at, such as violence, ambition and greed. For a time it
looked as if Julian would prevail over Augustine but it was
not to be. The Church in Rome wanted to emerge as a
centre of power and it needed a philosophy which made the
Church and the sacraments necessary to everyone. If you
show that everyone is sinful because everyone is carnal and
that sex is a sort of defining characteristic of the fallen, then
the church with its sacraments is much more necessary to
salvation.

It is wry now to remember the terror this [teaching] inspired:
the children who spent the night cruciform on the dormitory

floor after a 'dirty thought', the tears of shame and embarrassment in the confessional after teenage gropings at lights-out parties. But even while the terror gripped me, I was already doubtful. Although I could not have articulated it then as I can now, I sensed that the problem of human evil was more complex than concupiscence – at least in its narrow sexual definition.

From *Alone of All Her Sex*

The problem is you can't go on receiving the sacraments if you've committed a mortal sin and you can't be saved unless you're in a state of actual true contrition. This means you must promise never to do it again, so the minute you fall in love with someone this isn't really a state you can be in. The more tragic aspect of it concerns the question of abortion and contraception. Abortion is a sin which you commit once, or you hope you will commit only once. Then you repent of it and you can go to confession and resolve with all your heart never to do it again. You can then be saved, absolved and continue to be a Catholic. With contraception you can't in theory, although a lot of Catholics manage to square it with their conscience. In theory, contraception places you in a state of continual sin which should debar you from the sacraments.

The sanctions are quite frightening and we used to tot up the days in hell or in Purgatory. It was still in the era of indulgences when doing the Stations of the Cross would earn one so many days out of Purgatory. We had a grotto in the basement of the school and it was hung with rosaries that had been brought back from pilgrimages to different

Marian shrines. You obtained indulgences for all these pilgrimages, sometimes plenary indulgences, which meant that
all your days in Purgatory were cancelled. As a child I was
frightened of hell fire and purgatorial fire. In Italy there
are still images in the streets of the flames consuming the
souls. Even clergy go to Purgatory! And Mary presides over
the flames because she will save us. The mercy of Mary
was all to do with her ability to spare one this kind of torment. It wasn't just the afterlife and the pains of hell: we
were told that if we were naughty or wicked in this world we
would have a miserable life. Actually I think there's some
truth in that.

> Our holiness was a shallow affair, although most of us
> considered with complacent resignation the vocation to the
> cloister, which might suddenly come upon us. Other Christians
> are often shocked by Catholic frivolity. Our religion was
> certainly untroublesome because it consisted of simple
> certainties.
>
> From *Alone of All Her Sex*

I am glad of being a pre-Vatican II Catholic because of
the knowledge of the calendar and of saints' lives. There are
so many rules and rituals; I suppose there isn't really another
way of incorporating people into the faith. It is a language
and I think that actually a lot of Catholics felt that with the
easing of these rituals it is much harder to be a Catholic.
With an individualistic, humanist background one does
rebel against doing things by rote but there is a greater effi-
ciency in this idea that you follow instructions even if they

seem mindless because that is the way of making you a member of the body of the church.

It is this aspect of authority that is of course part of the Protestant reformation and rebellion against Catholicism. The Protestants wanted to place the individual conscience as the arbiter. For Catholicism, what is vitally important is the idea that authority does not lie within, it is not the inner voice but the outer voice, the voice of the Pope, the bishop, the priest and to some extent the nun.

The idea of being a member of this very ancient body of the Church gives you a greater historical perspective. It's also internationalist and so you belong to the world in an interesting way, it does tend to transcend local nationalism. I've often thought that the reason that there are so many writers who have been educated by nuns or priests is because of this idea of the daily examination of conscience. Writing is very close to the way that every Catholic child is asked to assess and try and make sense of the moral issues of life.

When I look back on it, I wonder why I felt so bitter and so frightened of it. It is difficult to pinpoint the strength of it, but in a way it is like a beloved authority figure of your youth that you cannot face. It is like a first husband or someone with whom you had an intense relationship and a deep acquiescence. It is hard to recognise continuity with that because it would imply another way of behaving; so you have to break away rather than continue.

After Vatican II

By the early 1960s most of the girls we spoke to were spreading their wings and making their way in the outside world and discovering for themselves whether or not it was that place of unbridled corruption and illicit pleasures the nuns had warned them of.

Too late to affect *their* education and attitudes; huge changes were on the way – changes that started with the election of Pope John XXIII in 1958. After only a year in office he announced that he intended to summon a Council – the first for nearly a hundred years – to consider the renewal of the Church and the question of 'Reunion'. Reunion, at this time, still implied that Anglicans and others who had left the 'real' church, should return to it forthwith. Nevertheless, the Second Ecumenical Council or Vatican II as it became known, was a unique event in ecclesiastical history which had far-reaching effects not only within the Basilica, but throughout the entire Catholic world. It is difficult, now, to imagine the momentous effect these years had upon ordinary people as they waited for the next holy 'law' to be issued from the Vatican. Whilst the preparations for the Council were taking place, the Archbishop of Canterbury paid a visit to the Pope in Rome. Although played down by the authorities as just a 'courtesy call', it was the first time since the Reformation, that an Archbishop of

Canterbury had visited the Pope. A Royal visit, in 1961, by
Queen Elizabeth and Prince Philip cemented the relationship and thousands of cinemagoers saw the event on
newsreel. The world was watching the Vatican with bated
breath. Pope John XXIII, an elderly man already in his sev-
enties when he came to office, was fast becoming an
internationally respected figure. When, in October 1962, he
officially opened the Second Ecumenical Council, Catholics
everywhere placed their trust in this warm-hearted man,
who they felt might break the mould of the harsh doctrine
they had endured for many years.

There was no one area of Catholic dogma singled out for
change. Vatican II was to be the 'Perestroika' of the
Catholic religion, sweeping away established thinking on
the Liturgy, on Ecumenism, on Divine Revelation, on
Religious Life, on Christian Education and on the Relation
of the Church to non-Christian religions. For the average
Catholic teenage girl, these pronouncements meant very
little. What she wanted to know was: would she be able to
wear her skirt more than three inches above the knee and
was a passionate kiss on the lips before marriage *still* a
mortal sin? The concerns of the nuns weren't quite along
the same lines, but they too had their queries. Would they
still have to wear a heavy and often restrictive habit? Would
they still be confined to teaching mainly girls?

Over the next decade the meanings behind the Vatican II
documents began to filter through. As with any laws, the
documents were open to a hundred and one different inter-
pretations and misinterpretations but the overall trend was
towards a liberalisation of the Catholic Church. The Mass

was no longer celebrated in Latin – a move that even today purists find disturbing. Nuns were not required to wear habits and schools headed by religious women *could* be co-educational. However, the most deeply felt and lasting effect is probably the most difficult for Catholics of the time to pinpoint. It was a general 'loosening up' of Catholic thinking. The Catechism – once learnt by rote under pain of punishment by all good Catholic children – was adapted and eventually given far less importance in religious tuition. Sex before marriage was, and still is, wrong in the eyes of the Church but it was no longer a tortuous moral issue for Catholic teenagers. Many of those 50s, convent girls, whose withdrawal from the Church coincided precisely with their first 'serious' boyfriend, perhaps need not have given up their faith with such haste.

Although radical, these changes took five, even ten years to really become part of the teaching system. The Catholic world was deeply affected by the death of their beloved Pope John in June 1963. Five hundred million Catholics worldwide mourned his death, not only for the loss of his homely, man-of-the-people approach, but for his brave vision of a new Catholicism. His death caught everyone by surprise. When the coronation of Pope Paul VI was organised at short notice, the ceremony had to be held outside the Basilica for the very first time in history, because the nave of the Basilica was filled with the seating, stands and paraphernalia of the Vatican Council. The Catholic community need not have feared – Pope Paul VI re-opened the Council and continued the reforms his predecessor had initiated.

For pre-Vatican II convent girls, the nuns' long flowing

habits had a memorable visual effect. Their presence could not be ignored. They were a constant reminder of an authority greater than the teacher and the school, and consequently often perceived as being more frightening. The leaving off of the habit was probably the most spectacular transformation that these girls would recognise in the wake of Vatican II. In fact, many Orders chose not to lose their habits at all, or until much later in the 1970s or 1980s. But many did return to plain clothes and many more adapted the dress, leaving off the wimple and veil and shortening the length of their skirts ...

The change for our order came quite recently, in 1985, when we came out of religious dress – or rather we had the option of coming out of religious dress if we wished to. But looking back, our foundress, the seventeenth century Englishwoman Mary Ward did not intend us to wear religious dress in the first place so this, in fact, is not an innovation; we're simply going back to an original concept. It wasn't without a certain amount of discussion because it is an important symbol to people. As a headmistress of a school where we have a lot of professional lay staff, I find my work easier without the habit. I used to find that because we were easily identifiable, parents would go up and talk to the nuns and perhaps miss important members of the lay staff such as the Deputy Headmistress.

Sister Mary Orchard (Institute of the Blessed Virgin Mary)
Headmistress of St Mary's, Ascot

I think it is important to have a visual presence of a religious Order in a school. Obviously there are many Orders around the country who don't wear habits and therefore they're not visibly sisters. I don't think they're any less religious or any less committed because of that. We, as an Order, happen to wear a habit and for us it is an important witness to what we're doing. But if we took off the habits tomorrow and wore ordinary clothing I don't think it would make any difference. If the children know we are committed and it is a Salesian school, then that is the important thing for us, not what we wear.

Sister Helen (Salesian Sisters) Headmistress,
St John Bosco's High School,
Croxteth, Liverpool

Since 1964 the number of nuns teaching in Catholic schools has dropped by 80 per cent. In 1990 just over a thousand* members of female religious orders were employed in schools and many of these work in Catholic rather than convent schools. There are many reasons for this decline; the religious vocation, like any other profession is vulnerable to a changing cultural and economic climate.

I think nuns have actually absorbed the challenge; their work is much harder today than it ever was, because people don't know where their values are. There are fewer teaching Sisters. There are different options for them. If you want to live a life of service and you want to devote your life to God, there are lots of different ways you can do that. It may be that the old convent-style vocation will be something that people rediscover later on but at the moment it's not attracting young people.

There are still communities that are busy and thriving.

*Figures from The Catholic Education Council 1990

They're not dying out although their vocations are fewer. But other communities do see their future as very worrying indeed. One Sister I was talking to recently said that they only have eighteen Sisters left in this country and they used to run several schools. Obviously they are looking at the future in a very bleak fashion. Some orders are still thriving, particularly major orders with a big educational input like the Dominicans; they're still very active in schools. Teaching is very person-intensive, so naturally they are looking to other areas of work which won't take so many personnel in one place. Running a school is a big enterprise.

I'm very concerned that there should be visible signs of the Church's involvement in education because people need it very badly. It's not that lay people can't do it – they can do it very well – but everybody needs to be in partnership and the more sisters there are in education, the better. Whether they have to do it strictly within the convent set-up is, in a way, less important. The many Sisters scattered throughout comprehensive and primary schools are a great gift to those schools. There's an assurance that the Church is there – there's a visible sign that people can see and relate to.

Kathleen O'Gorman Director,
The Westminster Diocesan Education Service

The most obvious change I've seen in my years here is the decline in the number of nuns at the school. When I came to the school in the mid-1950s they were a community of about sixty; now the community is twenty and only six of us work full-time in the school. We now have a very large professional, secular staff working with us. I think diversification is a good thing because members of our religious congregation are not necessarily going to find their vocation teaching in a school. Therefore, they must be allowed to use the God-given talents where they're best suited. More and more sisters are opting to work with the disadvantaged and the poor, with AIDS victims, in probation work and in a variety of community situations. Changes in the number of nuns in schools has inevitably meant a change of emphasis in the teaching. Yet, parents choosing to send their daughter to a convent school in the 1990s may still be looking for the traditional standards and a definite moral and spiritual input from the school . . .

When I was at St Mary's as a pupil we never thought in terms of careers; we thought only in terms of either marrying or becoming members of a religious congregation. They were really the only two options. I belonged to the last of that generation. As opportunities for women have expanded, so schools have had to meet the need for better educated women at university level and we have been much more aware of the importance of keeping up high standards.

Education has always been the work of the Church and it's very important work. The Catholic girls who come here are privileged in many senses – not just because they come from relatively well-off families, but because they come from families where values are very important. They are a privileged elite, but then, we expect an enormous amount of them when they go out into the world of work – in terms of multiplying the effects of the education they have received, spreading the Catholic faith and holding up moral standards.

Sister Mary Orchard (IVBM)
Headmistress, St Mary's, Ascot

I was at a comprehensive school in Glasgow and although it was a good school, there was never the communication between staff and pupils that I see here. There wasn't the freedom of speech, there wasn't the atmosphere. It was very much you went to school, you learnt and you went home again. There wasn't that healthy, friendly relationship between staff and pupils. That for me is the big difference. I think if we speak to children and treat them as human beings, as individuals, then they will respond.

Many Sisters feel that they can reach more people by doing community work. They can reach more children, more young people and perhaps have a greater input into their lives. I'm not sure I agree, but that's why many people go into that kind of work. We aim to work in areas where there is deprivation and children are in need of additional resources; that's why we've chosen this part of Liverpool. The aim is really to give the possibility of academic excellence, but at the same time helping them to become good people, with a knowledge of what their abilities are and to develop those. We have a strong feeling for the collective aspect of school, the family atmosphere. I know it's not a family, but we try to get the atmosphere whereby the children are free to speak to us. We try to make them realise that it is *their* school. It's not our school, it's not our possession, it's their school, it's their place of learning. It's their school when they're out on the streets, when they're on the bus, when they're talking to people outside, because if it is theirs they care for it.

Sister Helen (Salesian Sisters)
St John Bosco's High School, Croxteth, Liverpool

We do see this school as a Christian community. It doesn't mean we teach religion all the time, but we look at the whole package of education for children that is important for them in this day and age. I think there is a spirit that is in the convent community and flows into the school and is part of it. It is the spirit of accepting people, accepting every child for what they are. We have very high-powered children and very average children and you have to respect each girl with her own gifts and her own personality. I think they feel they are accepted and that they have caught, somehow, the idea that God is with them in their lives. I think this is why they feel something special in the school. I want them to take away a trust in God; and their trust is well placed, they are never alone. I want them to believe too, that we don't really forget them when we close the doors, we think of them. I would like them to feel that they can come back, in joyous moments and in sad moments and that there will be somebody here to receive them with welcome. It's friendship I think, friendship in the Lord and friendship with each other.

Sister Evelyn (Marist Sisters)
Headmistress, Marist Convent, Fulham, London

In the following chapters, we hear the voices of a new generation of convent girls. Their experience is the post-Vatican II convent school of the 1970s and 1980s, schools operating a regime that would be unrecognisable (and almost unbelievable) to the girls of the previous chapters.

Bernadine Corrigan

Bernadine Corrigan attended the Sacred Heart Convent in Hammersmith from the age of 11 to 16. She spent ten years as a secretary and another ten years as a stand-up comedienne, actress and writer. Then she returned to full-time study, gaining a First Class BA Hons Degree in Ancient Medieval History from London University, where she is currently reading for an MA in Hellenic Studies.

'Perhaps it's to do with coming from mixed parentage — I've got Protestant guilt and the Catholic work ethic. Which means you can sit on your arse all day and not feel guilty about it.'

I remember the school very well. I think I could still go round it with my eyes closed and know where everything is. It all comes flooding back. There were these cloisters which we used as a sort of recreation area. There was a ping-pong table, and we used to sit and eat chocolate biscuits and fool around. I don't think I ever felt it was a terribly holy place. I don't think I was ever really overawed by it. I mean when you're a teenager you're pretty callow and stupid and you just think this is the place where I go to school. It never struck me as being out of the ordinary. I remember we had a netball game once with another school and we had to ask them back to tea afterwards. So, they all came back to the cloisters and one of the girls from the other school said in a very hushed tone: 'Is this the church?' And I thought God, what a heathen, thinking this is the church! The cloisters were a bit gloomy though, for playtime.

There were a couple of nuns I remember well, who still wore the full habit. There was Sister Keeney who was brilliant. She taught us Maths and she was dreadfully sarcastic. And very dramatic too, the way she'd glide down the corridors like Darth Vadar with all this black stuff flowing behind her. In fact, she *sounded* a bit like Darth Vadar.

There was also Sister Bunbury, the headmistress. She was quite old, even then and she looked a bit like Malcolm

Muggeridge only with slightly more facial hair. There's a brilliant story that my sister told me – she was at the school a couple of years ahead of me – about Sister Bunbury. At the time there was a drive on to collect milk bottle tops which miraculously turned into Guide Dogs for the blind. Well apparently it wasn't going too well and we weren't collecting very many, so one day at assembly, Sister Bunbury stood up and addressed the girls. She had an enormous long tongue that used to sweep the ground in front of her as she spoke and her veil was always falling off, so she kept shoving it back on while she was talking. And she said: 'Girls, girls, we're really not collecting very many milk bottle tops and so I want you all to go home and tell your mothers to make love to the milkman . . .' All the girls absolutely fell about. Of course she meant just fluttering your eyelashes over the top of your fan, but it just conjured up this lovely picture of all these good Catholic mothers desperately rogering the milkman for an extra pint of goldtop!

The younger nuns were a bit more trendy. They didn't wear habits – they wore Marks and Spencer's outfits with American tan tights. I remember one in particular who hadn't actually taken her final vows. We were doing a class one day and we started talking to her about when she was going to finally become a nun and we started trying to dissuade her from taking the vows. Someone asked her what she would miss most about her previous life and she spoke with a terribly posh accent and said: 'Well of course I'll miss my horse . . .' We all came from council estates in west London and we couldn't really connect with that. So, she started to try and recoup a bit of lost ground and said:

'Well, of course also I miss "cheps" . . .' Again it was the sound of 13 and 14 year olds rolling in the aisles. She stopped saying chaps and tried 'blokes' because she thought it was more the kind of thing we'd say. Poor soul. Actually I think I'm right in saying that shortly afterwards she did leave the sisterhood and took up with her horses and chaps again . . . probably more horses than chaps.

It wasn't a closed order and they did get out and about. It was very difficult for them because they were trying to push a dogma that doesn't seem to apply to most of us now. They used to try and tell us in a very sort of vague way not to have sex before we were married, but I think they knew they were on to a loser because we all thought it was a terribly *good* idea to get as much snogging in as possible.

Nuns really don't have the same responsibilities as people outside. When it came to things like school uniform, which was so expensive, it didn't bother them because they don't have those sort of expenses. I think in that way they are slightly distanced from what's going on in real life. Our uniform was quite straightforward, royal blue with a cream coloured blouse but the regulation cardigans and jumpers were very expensive. You could buy the second-hand version from a lady in the cloisters, but if you were seen going there everyone knew you were poor. I didn't really mind, but we used to go to Martin Fords which had very close copies of the originals in a nice attractive nylon. By the time I got to the fifth year, I had the elbows sticking out of my cardigan. First of all it was my jumper, then I wore the cardigan over it to cover the hole and then I wore that through too. The teachers would occasionally stop me and say:

Bernadine why are you such a mess? And I'd say it was because my parents couldn't afford to buy me new ones because we were very poor. Then, of course, I'd go home and my parents would say: Why don't you go and get a new cardigan for God's sake you look disgusting!

There wasn't really a stigma against being poor because we were mostly working-class girls anyway. My father was a Catholic born and bred and his family were staunch Catholics. My mother was Church of England, but she converted to Catholicism because she wanted to marry him and it was easier to do that, not because of any great conversion. Neither of them were terribly bothered about religion, but I suppose it was still the done thing to send your daughters to a convent school. They are very good schools, that's the point. If you can't afford to pay for education then Catholic schools tend to provide you with a rather good one for free. That's how I ended up going and it was a good choice. We've got some relatives in the religious orders. My father's cousin is a priest and my aunt is a Reverend Mother at a convent in Epsom. I'm glad she hasn't seen my act, she'd never speak to me again.

Bernadine's act includes some convent sequences.

'I did go to convent school. It was an unusual convent school actually because the nuns had been trained by the SAS – they were called The Little Sisters of Perpetual Extermination – they wore flak habits. There were a few plain clothes, undercover nuns – you could spot those ones, they kept their bibles in shoulder holsters. We had a great respect for these women, because when they came into the classroom we had to lie face down on the floor with our hands behind our heads . . .'

I have to admit, my act is totally made up. The Sacred Heart was actually quite mild by the time I got here in the 70s – I don't know what it was like in the 50s and 60s. It wasn't terribly oppressive and the nuns certainly didn't fill me with guilt. But, of course, it's not funny to go on stage and say: 'Hello, I went to a convent school and it was all right . . .' Not much of a joke there really. People expect you to have had a terrible time at a convent school. It makes them feel better, I don't know why. I'm afraid my act is complete fantasy.

I'm a total atheist now. I never feel I've got Catholic guilt. Perhaps it's to do with coming from mixed parentage – I've got Protestant guilt and the Catholic work ethic, which means you can sit on your arse all day and not feel guilty about it. I've never had any traumas about it. I'm quite glad about that really because you do get a lot of 'professional Catholics' who get very tedious about how dreadful their upbringing was. It hasn't had that effect on me at all.

I didn't know I was going to be a comedienne when I was at school. I told them I was going to be an actress and they weren't desperately pleased. They said: at least stay for your 'A' levels because Pauline Collins did and she's done very well. They were quite right of course. I should have stayed. Instead I went off and got a job as a typist which was going to be something to fall back on, which it was – for the next ten years.

I don't know what I'd do if I had children. I don't have any faith at all now, but on the other hand I object to paying school fees. I don't know what I'd do. I'd probably be hypocritical and send them to the Sacred Heart. I probably won't be allowed to after they've read this ...

Ellie Laine

Born in 1963, Ellie Laine went to St Mary's Convent School in Woodford, Essex from the age of four to fourteen. It has now burnt down: 'Nothing to do with me, honest.' She was an imaginative child, often in trouble for telling tall tales. She describes herself as a raunchy comedienne and has become something of a tabloid star, an image she says has been helped rather than hindered by her convent background. She now lives in Florida.

'I did want to be a nun for a while — everyone hoots with laughter when I tell them. Nuns were terribly glamorised, like Debbie Reynolds as the singing nun which I thought was wonderful and very romantic.'

When the media and newspapers found out I was an ex-convent girl they had a field day. I didn't mean to tell them, it just slipped out, but they thought it was hysterical. I think it was because it was so much in contrast to my sexy, raunchy image and the outfits that I wore, but that's the way I am. I looked like that. I couldn't help it. I was well endowed at a very early age with blonde hair. They thought it was so incongruous, but I'm not ashamed of having been a convent girl and I certainly don't apologise for it.

I went to my convent school when I was very young and stayed until I was fourteen – so they had me for the best part of my school life. At fourteen I was finally asked to leave; I wouldn't say I was exactly expelled – it was more a case of if I hadn't left voluntarily then I would have been expelled.

Looking back I have a little bit of sympathy for the nuns because I wasn't an easy child – I probably put most of them off children for life. They were very strict and I found that hard to deal with. We had these set little uniforms all navy blue, very demure, and awful regulation knickers which we used to call bumbags. Basically they tucked down over your bum and came up to your neck. As we got older we obviously didn't like wearing them. We used to have knicker inspections when, at the drop of a hat, the nuns would march into the room, we'd all have to stand to attention and then lift up our skirts in order to prove we had on the correct knickers. It was very bizarre. Word used to get round: 'Change your knickers, girls! and we'd all have a spare pair in our satchels.'

The school was a bit like Colditz; it had beautiful grounds but it had these great big high walls to keep us away from the rest of the world. I used to break out and climb up the walls, but at the top there were these spikes which I had to get over to lower myself down into the street. It was quite a drop and one day I got my bumbags caught on the spikes and I was suspended on the street side by my knickers until a passer-by alerted one of the nuns. I was lifted down and it was highly embarrassing. I was told I was an evil child and marched in front of Reverend Mother and suspended for a week. That didn't seem to be much of a punishment to me.

One lasting memory is of the food. They used to cook this fish in milk and it used to come up grey and scummy with brown bubbles in it. We also used to have tinned tomatoes which went on the plate with everything else so it was all pink. Then they'd add mashed potatoes which used to soak up this pink, grey, milky fishy substance and it made me feel ill. I'd say: 'I can't eat it,' and they'd say: 'You must, for the poor children in this world. You're a very wicked child.' I actually tried to post my dinner to the poor children one day which didn't go down too well.

When I was very young and very naughty, I used to get put in the cupboard quite a bit. There were these huge cupboards which were used for stationery, and if I was very bad I used to get locked in there. It got to the point that I'd no sooner walk into a lesson and I'd be put in the cupboard.

One time, it was the school sports day and I went into the changing rooms where all the little shoe bags were hanging on little hooks. I don't know what made me do it, but I sat through the lunch break and knotted every single shoebag into a double knot. I mean there were 300 bags! Of course, the sports day had to be called off because no one could get their plimsolls and games kits out.

Another time when I was eight years old I had to have an operation – nothing major, but it did require stitches on my side. Nobody believed me at school because I only had a small plaster over it. It was end of term sports day and I told the nuns I couldn't take part but they didn't believe me. I went into a race, fell over and split my side open. I've actually got quite a big scar on my side and it took a long time to heal.

I was a real tomboy – I actually climbed the statue of the Virgin Mary in the chapel which I was very good at getting up but not at getting down. Another time I locked all the nuns in this old-fashioned music room where they used to assemble for discussions. I could hear them shouting: 'You evil child, let us out!' I don't know how they knew it was me, but they were there for five hours while the whole school ran riot. That was probably the most significant factor towards my being asked to leave. I think they were glad to get rid of me.

I did go to confession which is very difficult when you are young: I really didn't know what to confess although I knew it was important to confess all your sins. I was a very imaginative child and if I thought I hadn't done anything I used to make things up, and very juicy stuff too. I didn't know what was considered worth confessing.

The education was good, but limited. I found when I left the school I was very behind other kids. We used to do old-fashioned things like needle-work and tapestries. It was very narrow. I had an enquiring mind and used to read geographical and scientific magazines. I was very confused when I read about evolution and dinosaurs and eggs and how man evolved and all the different stages that we've been through. I couldn't understand the religious part of it all. We were told that God made the world in seven days and that it all started with Adam and Eve, and I just couldn't work out where the dinosaurs fitted in. I can remember asking about dinosaurs and the nuns couldn't answer.

One of my friends who sat next to me in class was left-handed. The left hand was associated with the sign of the devil and the nuns felt she shouldn't be left-handed, that she should learn to write with her right hand. She used to get rapped across the knuckles and she had to sit at the back of the class and trace copperplate writing – relearning to write. Of course she never did and she became totally backward. It was most important that we had nice, feminine hand-writing. I've got very weird writing now because my natural writing was slightly wild and scrawly, but we were made to sit there and trace copperplate writing so that we would all write the same. We were cloned. There was nothing finer than to be a good mother and have children, which is great, but there was no career emphasis.

Looking back I think the discipline has probably stood me in good stead for what I do. We learnt to be very self-contained and that is a wonderful thing in show business. With my personality I didn't go under. I didn't totally conform. I can be true to do what I want. I think, well, I've come this far, I've stood up against authority this far. Having said that I'm still reduced to a little girl when I see a nun. It's yes, Sister, no Sister. It still comes back to me. I remember one show I did – we had all the tables laid out with place names and the people working with me swapped them all and wrote 'Sister Thérèse' and 'Reverend Mother'. They knew I used to go round and read the name tags to involve people in my act. I started reading them and I was terrified – I was thinking can I clean up my act? I thought I just can't go on tonight, the whole front row is religious. So, it does come back on me. But, I'm very proud of what I do; there are certain nuns who I am sure would probably laugh, who have a great sense of humour.

I did want to be a nun for a while – everyone hoots with laughter when I tell them. Nuns were terribly glamorised, like Debbie Reynolds as the singing nun which I thought was wonderful and very romantic. Films like *The Sound of Music*, I thought were just great. We all had great ideals and images. There were some very sweet nuns who were lovely. I did go through a phase where I thought I would like to be like them. I was very kindly told I probably wasn't nun material, for which I am forever grateful.

I don't think I'd have any qualms about sending my children to a convent school, just because it was a convent school but I would certainly make sure it was what I wanted for them and that they were happy. I did have problems at my particular school; possibly if I'd gone to another convent it would have been fine and I'd have been thoroughly happy. My mother went to St Mary's and she had the most wonderful time, but of course she had different teachers. She thought: It was so wonderful I'll send my own daughter there. She couldn't see I was having problems because her experience had been good. When I was actually thrown out of the convent my mother was shocked and very apologetic. I was a huge embarrassment. I think she wanted me to follow through – she was actually headgirl and she wanted to become a nun and everything. I don't think she quite understood that I found it very difficult although I think she accepted it eventually. But I'm fairly open about children's schooling generally and if there was a convent in my area and it was a nice school I would send mine there.

Mary O'Hara

Mary O'Hara was born in 1969, the third of seven children born to Roman Catholic parents, living in Belfast, Northern Ireland. Although she was one of the brightest pupils at her junior school, St Joseph's Primary, she astonished her teachers by failing her 11+ and went to St Louise's Comprehensive College, the largest single sex school in Europe, with some 2,500 pupils. Mary was the first person from the school to win a place at Oxbridge and graduated in social and political science from Magdalene College, Cambridge in 1991. She went on to study at the University of Michigan before returning to England to work for Capital Radio. She has since co-written a feature film screenplay and is currently a journalist on the *Guardian* and is based in London.

'Some of my fondest memories up until now are from school. I had a really good time ... my teachers helped me through a lot of difficult times, times when I didn't believe in myself.'

I suppose I'm from a typical Catholic family. We are seven children and most of them are younger than me. There is no history of education in our family so at first I don't think they grasped what my coming to Cambridge meant. I was the first person in the family to go to university and now they're really proud of me. And I'm really proud of them.

The first school I went to was St Joseph's Primary School, on the Grosvenor Road in Belfast. I went there from about the age of eight and it probably set me up for life actually. It was a really, really good school. The teachers there were something else, and I still keep in touch with them. They coached me through, to get my 11+ – but they were so understanding when I didn't get it. I thought I'd never be able to do 'A' levels because I'd failed it. But as I was leaving they advised me to go to St Louise's, and on the basis of their advice, I went, and I've done all right. Even people who've passed their 11+ want to go there – as well as middle-class people. Well, in west Belfast anyone with a job is middle-class, but you know what I mean!

St Louise's is twenty-five or thirty years old now, the largest single sex school in western Europe. It's very large, around 2,500 pupils and a really large teaching staff of around 126. It's a Catholic school, on the Falls Road, and an excellent school because it provides facilities that a lot of the other schools in Northern Ireland don't provide. I followed an academic course, but I could do commercial subjects and typewriting as well. They cater for all sorts of abilities and have children from eleven to eighteen.

When you get to the sixth form, the options are opened even wider. You can do so much. It's got an excellent drama department. The teachers are very supportive and it's actually quite well known. Another nice thing about the sixth form is that there is much more freedom. There's also more responsibility, but overall it does give you a lot more confidence. One thing I've noticed about people in west Belfast is that they're not very good where authority is concerned They're not very confident about themselves, whereas the school taught us to believe in ourselves, to believe that we could stand up and say things and do things that nobody else could.

The increased responsibility came in a variety of ways: the sixth form had various duties, like taking assemblies and looking after the younger pupils – but at the same time we were treated as adults. We were no longer pupils, we had our own section of the school. And whatever we did we got thanked for it.

There are a lot of schools on the Falls Road and none of them have managed to accomplish what St Louise's has. I'm very proud of it because a lot of people who go there don't start off in life with the best of opportunities, there aren't very many doors open to them. It's not like any other educational institution because the teachers are so enthusiastic; they'll stay in after school, they'll give up half an hour of their lunch to look after the younger pupils, they'll sit around with you – but they'll always push you that much harder. You get all sorts of teachers, all sorts of pupils, but for some reason it seems to work, and a lot of people come out of that place successful. My generation have never known anything but the Troubles in west Belfast, so we really needed something stable to give us a chance. Every school has to have rules and regulations and I know that at times in my school life I hated them, they just got on my nerves. But the rules weren't so imposing that you felt you were restricted in any way. You could see the logic of them and as you get older you tend to see the logic a bit more, you no longer feel hostile.

A lot of the fellas that grow up around that area really don't have much hope. The schools don't push them that hard, and they can easily get sucked in to whatever's going on in the streets. For children of my generation the streets could be quite rough, like most inner cities. When children leave school they're susceptible to pretty bad influences educationalists can't really do much about. The problems often start with unstable home backgrounds which the teachers have to try and cope with. Although it takes special skills, the teachers aren't trained.

Our school had all sorts of facilities, and if you were aware of what was on offer, of what it could do for you, then you could get somewhere. We had assemblies in the morning, when you had to be in fifteen minutes earlier and most people did turn up. The assemblies were lovely because the students were able to take part and half the time wrote their own prayers, so that we were talking about things we wanted to talk about. The teachers let us do it, and let us sing hymns that we wanted to sing. So you didn't mind turning up early, or any of the other rules. I suppose I could be a bit biased when it comes to Sister Genevieve, the headmistress, because she's a very good friend of mine as well, but she practically built the school and she's completely devoted to it.

When I first arrived at the school it was quite daunting. I remember she got up to speak at the first year assembly and it was quite nerve-racking because she was up on another level and seemed quite dominant, in control. But you found out after a while that she was actually quite approachable. Once I got to the sixth form I got to know her much better. She really took a personal interest in the sixth formers and pushed you for whatever you wanted to do afterwards. Whatever your career prospects were, she'd always be there to help you out.

I knew I would do quite well at 'A' Levels, but I never thought I'd ever get into Cambridge. The vice-principal called me into her office one day and said: 'We think you should apply.' So I thought, okay, I haven't a hope of getting in, but what the hell, I'll just fill in the form – and forgot about it.

When I came up for the interviews the school was really helpful, because I was so nervous. Afterwards I believed there was no way I'd get in because I'd messed it all up. But all the school said was, 'Well you went and you did your best and that's all that can be asked.' I thought that was really sweet because I knew they would have liked people from the school to get into Oxbridge. It was the same reaction as

when I was worried about my 'A' Levels: 'As long as you've
done your best . . .'

When I got my provisional offer from Cambridge I
wasn't quite sure about whether to go, because I knew nothing about the place. I didn't think I'd fit in and I didn't
know what the people here were like. Sister Genevieve and
the other teachers knew I was very unsure, but she just said:
'Go, give it a try, we'll be with you all the way.' And they
have been. The vice-principal and Sister Genevieve have
been over to visit me while I've been here and we keep in
touch the whole time.

It's all so completely different here. Magdalene College
was all male until the year I arrived, so I was one of the first
thirty-six women – a bit of a change from being in an institution with 2,500 women. That was quite a shock!

Studying politics and sociology here I've had a really
amazing two years. It's done a lot for my confidence as well
but the experience I had at St Louise's really helped me
out. I feel I can meet different people and get on with them.
If you live in west Belfast you don't meet a terribly wide
variety of people but when you come here, you do. Then,
all of a sudden, you realise people aren't that different after
all.

The religious stuff wasn't shoved down our throats.
There was a large religious element but it wasn't so much
Catholic oriented. Going to a Catholic school on the Falls
Road in Belfast, you'd think, that's a Catholic ghetto
anyway, you're not going to get any other religions open to
you. In fact, it emphasised all religions. It was a Catholic
school, the Catholic religion was taught, but we were also

aware of what else was going on. We had various societies and we met with Protestant schoolchildren and chatted to them. We weren't isolated, although it would have been so easy to cut us off from people in other religions. We had ecumenical services where we met clergy from various different Protestant religions, and we had moral philosophy classes where we discussed moral issues. It wasn't all seen from a Catholic viewpoint, we were encouraged to voice our opinions in class – and we weren't penalised for it. Some people believe that in Catholic schools the Catholic religion is all you're taught, that you're not given a chance to do or say anything else. I don't know about other convent schools, but ours certainly wasn't like that. There were a lot of people there who were quite religious, some who weren't, but I certainly didn't feel restricted.

We were taught traditional prayers and we studied things from critical standpoints to a large extent. As soon as you were capable of reading the gospels, you were made aware of inaccuracies and encouraged to compare them. Things weren't drummed into us, it wasn't mechanical the way it would have been maybe twenty or thirty years ago. We weren't told *this* is what you believe, you've no choice in the matter. Having spoken to my parents and grandparents about the way they were taught religion, it's very different. I'm not particularly religious, although I get on okay with it.

We had a sort of cross-school link between schools of different religions. The children meet up at weekends and have a youth club. That isn't educationally based but the educationalists work in association with it, one of the few ways that they can do something about the problem of getting kids off the streets.

Other extra-curricular activities like drama give the children a positive interest – and that's what you need because the whole environment is so negative. It's really quite sad, because the people are so lovely.

Leaving St Louise's is really a day to remember, because everybody feels so affectionate towards the place. My most lasting memory will be its warmth I think, a really nice feeling. Some of my fondest memories up until now are from school. I had a good time and am good friends with a few teachers. They helped me through many difficult times, times when I didn't believe in myself. Everybody there helps everybody else out.

Chantal Coady

Chantal Coady was born in 1959 and joined St Leonard's, Hastings, Sussex in 1969 moving on to its senior school, Mayfield, until the age of 16. The school was at the time run by nuns of the order of The Holy Child of Jesus. Chantal went on to study textile design and business before setting up her own company, Rococo, in 1983, selling fine organic chocolate from her shop in the King's Road, Chelsea. She is an active promoter of the *Campaign for Real Chocolate* and has written several books, including *Real Chocolate* (Quadrille, 2003), which includes recipes and anecdotes relating to her convent days. Chantal is married with two children, Emilia aged 4 and Fergus, aged 6 and lives in London.

'There were so many petty rules that needed to be broken. You couldn't beat the system totally, but you got very good at strategic management. Learning to challenge authority, that's what I've taken from my convent education.'

Interestingly when I meet 'old girls' now, when they come into the shop, and perhaps they've read articles about me, they talk about the convent experience. I remember one girl came in and said 'I'm really glad that you talked about those days, because I just began to think I'd imagined the whole thing. It was just like a bad dream, but you telling your story has actually made me realise that it did happen.'

It was a horrific experience – being a nine year old and far away from your parents in a very cold environment, it was a physically cold and an emotionally cold place – with this alien set of rules which you couldn't understand why they were there. And this system of extreme suppression – the power that the nuns had was all consuming, you could feel it all around you – and you couldn't challenge it except in small ways. It was like being in prison, you had no rights and very few material possessions and you were being constantly spied upon. It was a very cold psychological environment.

The reason for going to St Leonard's was that my parents were Catholic. My father was a more fervent Catholic than my mother and he was a doctor specialising in tropical medicine and was always posted abroad. At the age of 9 we were living in Kuwait and there wasn't a school we could go to there. If we'd been living in England they wouldn't have sent us away.

There are five of us and we all got sent off one by one. The family is a sandwich with the two brothers on the outside and the three sisters in the middle (in terms of age) and I'm the absolute middle. Being in the middle meant I always had one or other sister at school with me. So, I always had one of them to back me up, whereas they were isolated.

I remember going to visit before I went there and walking down to the beach and getting tar on my clothes. There was a very nice nun who told me I needed olive oil to rub it off. She went and got some olive oil and rubbed it off. And it all seemed very nice and the summer uniforms were very pretty, pale blue and white. When I actually arrived I think the biggest shock was lying in bed on the first night and just chattering away naturally to the other girls . . . and no one answered me. Within a minute a nun burst in and bellowed at us – it just hadn't occurred to me that this could be a punishable offence. One of the times I was caught talking I was marched down in my pyjamas to the study hall where the older girls were still doing their homework and I had to walk onto the stage and be publicly humiliated and made to write a hundred lines. What was all that about really?

I never learned to knuckle down. The punishments were always psychological. There was this feeling of 'all seeing, all knowing' – they seemed to have spies everywhere. You couldn't get away with doing anything. Possibly they had recruited more timid girls to act as spies for them. Who knows? They censored your letters home – girls were not allowed to write bad things about the school because, so we were told, our parents didn't want to hear it. The thinking was that the parents had made great sacrifices to send us to this school. Often there were genuine reasons why girls had been sent there – broken marriages and so on. But my family were a normal, functional family and whenever there were problems, even from a long distance they would try and intervene and sort things out.

There was one occasion involving my younger sister. There was a nun showing some parents around and walking through the dormitory she opened the door of a blanket cupboard and there was my sister, aged 9, and her friend playing in the cupboard, because it was so cold everywhere else. The nun said 'oh isn't that sweet' but after the parents had gone she summoned them to her room and gave them the most almighty 'blowing up' as we called it. Then she wrote to my parents in Kuwait and said 'your daughter is having an unnatural relationship with this girl and we want to keep them separate – and not allow them to be friends.' My parents got out all my sister's old reports and photocopied them and sent them back to the nuns saying 'we just don't believe this, this is not the daughter we know and for you to be suggesting that she is having some sort of lesbian relationship at the age of 9 is absurd.' But they still tried to drive a wedge between my sister and her friend, although not very successfully.

The building was Victorian. It looked rather like Colditz, a very austere building perched on the top of the hill. There was a tunnel which led from one building to another and I often have nightmares that I'm back in that building. The tunnel had grotto alcoves all along it – where there had been statues and a huge picture of the foundress, Cornelia Connelly which had these eyes that followed you as you walked along. We used to tell each other there were people buried in the alcoves – it was very damp, dark and spooky and we'd run through it to get between the buildings. That was one of the places we'd be lined up in the middle of the night as a punishment and the lights would be turned off. Another was the winding staircase of the church tower. We had to stand still in complete silence until this completely stark, raving mad nun came back to let us out.

The nuns wore habits – the older generation still wore the great long flowing habits with the full wimples. But by my day, the younger nuns had started to wear shorter ones, above the ankle and half way down below the knee. They definitely liked the new dress code and by the time I was at Mayfield, some of the nuns would buy their clothes from Jaeger, which we didn't think was very unworldly of them. And gradually, they stopped wearing the veils altogether and were pretty much 'plain clothes'. I would think it was about 60/40 lay teachers to nuns, but the nuns ruled the roost.

The headmistress of St Leonard's had apparently been in a concentration camp. She was born Jewish and had been under that regime in Nazi Germany. Later she converted to Catholicism and became a nun. I think that a lot of where she was coming from was due to the way she herself had been treated. She disappeared – we didn't know where but we thought she might have had a nervous breakdown. Many years later, she reappeared as a support worker for the Terrence Higgins Trust doing a piece on Thought for the

Day on Radio 4 – I almost died . . . that voice . . . We called
her Fish because she looked like a fish. She was the scariest
of the nuns.

She made such an impression on me. My abiding
memory is of having a silver puzzle ring confiscated and
when I went to ask for it back, she sat across from me and
just said 'I chucked it'. I was really angry about it. I don't
think I was a particularly naughty child, but it was not
hard to regularly break the rules. Coming from a big family
I was quite confident. I was used to organising people and
I was probably a bit of a ringleader. My older sister had in
her report 'quietly obstinate' – she was just a bit more
subtle about her naughtiness. She was held up as a good
example.

At Mayfield, the headmistress seemed to me a much
weaker figure – we never felt really challenged by her, perhaps because you'd been through the St Leonard's
experience and came out the other side. I remember one
nun called Sister Theresa Joseph (known as 'TJ') who
seemed benign and was always kind to me. She had back
problems and it was always stressed how much pain she
endured and how she never complained about the pain.
She was such a stoic.

The nuns were a mixture of backgrounds. The Irish nuns
tended to be lowly ones and there was a great system of
hierarchy there. Apparently some of them came from very
good families who had sacrificed huge amounts of worldly
wealth to the convent as a dowry and then they were always
on the top rung of the ladder. And then there was one nun
who was extremely bad tempered, but I always felt really

sorry for her because she looked so downtrodden and got to do all the menial jobs.

One of the children's fathers was the famous 1960s conman who was in jail for insurance fraud and we always wondered who paid her fees. My parents were rather shocked that they took this girl in and, on one side, you could say they were being rather charitable, but on the other ... The Marcos children from the Philippines were also pupils and they had bodyguards who lived in the village – the younger girl was my contemporary. The Marcos family would send presents for all the children – such as a huge chest of cutlery – which would never reach us and rumours abounded about what happened to them.

The day was governed by bells. We didn't have to go to church every day unless it was a feast day. Bells to get up, get dressed, go down to breakfast, bells for lessons. We had to go to mass on Sunday. I don't have clear memories of religion at school, paradoxically. I had done my Holy Communion before I arrived at St Leonard's so I already knew my catechism, etc. It was at the time – around 1969 – when it was changing over from the Latin Mass to English.

I was good at art and they used to ask me to design posters for the school so I suppose from that point of view they did try and channel some of my creative energy. It was a very academic school, and that didn't suit me particularly well. I managed to get through without doing too much work but I wasn't gripped or excited by any of the academic things that were going on.

At nine or ten I remember these little booklets we were given about starting periods and so on – we never talked about it, we were just expected to read it. It was always a Catholic interpretation of the Facts of Life and they had nothing to do with sex at all. Periods and having babies were about marriage, and of course, marriage was about having babies. There was no mention of fun. I remember thinking, that couldn't be all there was to it.

I remember always feeling cold and hungry at school. Because I came from warmer climates and we were allowed only three blankets, I just remember always feeling cold. We wore the summer uniform in the summer term, even if it was snowing outside. And the food was absolutely appalling and I just had this craving for chocolate. I'd stock up on the shopping day, but being me I'd just eat it all on one day and then crave for it all week. My mother used to, very sweetly, send me food parcels to coincide with the day when I had usually hit my lowest point. It made a big impression on me and I'm sure that was a motivation for starting the chocolate shop. Even now, after running the business for 20 years, if I'm away from chocolate for a long time and there's no way of getting any, that feeling comes back – it's my security blanket.

The school uniform was vast. There were over-underpants which had the school badge on and under-underpants – which was in case you got run over. Of course, we used to customise the uniform and we rolled up our skirts as short as we could because minis were in fashion. In the fifth form you could wear socks, flesh coloured tights or navy blue tights. For prize day I wore the dark blue ones and I remember my best friend's mother saying 'she looks like a tart in those tights'. As time progressed, we were allowed to wear our own clothes at weekends. The effects of Vatican II were beginning to kick in and also they needed to attract more pupils.

There were organised socials in the fifth and sixth form and boys from a local Catholic school were shipped in, who either had glasses, spots or a limp – or sometimes all three. There were no perfect specimens to be had. For me they were of no interest whatsoever because my elder sister and brother had already left school and had a cool group of friends. When I went home I would go out and party with them. At school they even had a screen in the corner where boys and girls could go and have a discreet kiss. With a nun standing in the corner like a sentinel on duty! I remember thinking how sad they were.

At sixteen, when I was doing my 'O' levels, I went to confession but I always had problems thinking what to say. So I said, 'Father, I missed mass because I was studying for my exams.' He said 'You are a wicked child, a wicked, wicked sinner! Now go to the back of the church and say 50 Hail Marys and 50 Our Fathers.' And I thought, if I do that, they'll probably think I slept with the priest at least, or murdered someone! So I just walked straight out of the confessional and straight out of the church and that was my divorce from the Catholic Church.

I want to pass on to my children a value system, but not the one I got at school. They always imposed on you this thing about 'being on your honour' and in a way that was slightly sinister – the way children buy in to that and don't have any choice but to behave in the way that they've prom-ised to do. But in another way, society needs to have those honourable codes and most kids grow up believing that they don't have to be on their honour to do anything.

Perverse as it may seem, I decided to baptise my own children and bring them up as Catholics, because it stood me in very good stead. I think it is excellent to have a secure framework to grow up in and you can question it as you grow up and kick against it if you want to. It's much healthier to have an institution like that than to have nothing. I think the idea that you have no religious upbringing and then suddenly decide to become a Buddhist is rather bizarre. It's good to have something to start off with.

I started going to church again when the children were born. You just reappraise your whole life and your value systems. When I went to baptise my children, I went to see the priest and he said, so tell me about your relationship with the Catholic Church and I said 'I'm very lapsed'. And he said, 'No, my dear, we don't say lapsed, we say you went into retirement.' And I told him all about the school and the nuns and he said 'Oh those nuns have got a lot to answer for, but I'm glad you've decided to come out of retirement.' I didn't have to pretend.

The Catholic school across the road from where we live refused to take my son because we don't go to their church – we go to one in a different diocese. And the nun told us it would be unacceptable because we'd be paying our money into different coffers. Unbelievable. This is a nun speaking who is supposed to be about poverty and charity. They were relentless.

I made a lot of good friends at school and it gave me a strength of character that maybe I wouldn't have had. The learning to bend the rules, learning to challenge authority – that's what I've taken from my convent education. There were so many petty rules that I felt needed to be broken, like the rule about not being allowed to run, or talk after lights out. You couldn't beat the system totally, but we got good at strategic management – working out how to break as many rules as we could without being found out, that became our goal. We weren't allowed to go out shopping, but we'd give money to the priest and say 'Father Flood, please, we're having a midnight feast, would you buy us some cream cakes?' And he would go and get them and bring them in! There was one time we climbed through the windows of the cookery building and made ourselves pancakes, but we would always do it so that no one would know we'd been there. We'd never take too much flour or sugar, and we'd always leave it completely neat and tidy.

I don't think I was damaged by it, but I would not send my children to a boarding school unless they really, really begged to go. The Billy Bunter and Famous Five stories glamorise it in a way and children think that's all it is – midnight feasts and fun. For me it was a kind of challenge to survive it and to make it fun and in a lot of ways it was a really formative experience. But, I remember other girls being really crushed by it and that was sad.

I still go to St Ethelreda's, the oldest Catholic church in England, which has a beautiful sung mass in Latin, and for me it is just a little refuge of peace and quiet which I enjoy very much. I once heard someone say that when you hear sublime music, or see great works of art, they transport you to another level – it proves that God must exist. I grew up in a time of great change in the Roman Catholic church, and consequently I never learnt the Latin mass properly and I'm pretty rusty on the English one now, but I still enjoy the rare moments of stillness that I find in that church.

Marian Keyes

Marian Keyes was born in the west of Ireland in 1963. She attended a convent school in South County Dublin, went on to college and obtained a law degree. Her twenties were spent working in London, in a variety of jobs and during this time her life long low self-esteem gradually mutated into a drinking problem. After a suicide attempt at 30 she went into rehab and afterwards wrote her first book, *Watermelon*, published in 1995. To date her books have sold over 8 million copies worldwide. She now lives in Dublin with her English husband, Tony.

'There are a lot of robust people who came through the convent system and it didn't take a lump out of them, but I think if you were in any way sensitive or a bit more fragile, as I was, the nuns had the capacity to do enormous damage.'

One of my most vivid memories was on a school trip to France. We were in Paris, driving in a coach through Pigalle, the red-light district. All around us were posters and photos advertising 'le sexy-striptease' and similar – and the minute the nuns spotted this, they nearly had a vapour. I remember one nun, running up and down, trying to pull down those little blinds you have on a coach – totally useless – so that we wouldn't see. It was typical of their behaviour – trying to pretend the real world didn't exist and turning themselves into objects of ridicule in the process.

Thinking about it now, I imagine some of the nuns had been boarders at school as children and most became nuns at a very early age so they would never have experienced healthy relationships. As a result – in my opinion, and I can only speak for myself and these particular nuns – they didn't ever mature. Many of them were astonishingly spiteful and on the same emotional maturity level as the girls they were teaching. This idea that wisdom is something that is delivered from on high? Well, in my opinion, it's not. Apart from a few, very special people, wisdom is something that is acquired slowly, over the course of a lifetime, by engaging with other human beings, encountering different types of people and discovering how you interact; by confrontation, forgiveness and living. I don't think these women had the opportunity to grow as human beings, so I don't think they were fully rounded, but of course I didn't know that at the time.

I don't have vivid first impressions, perhaps because one of my father's aunts was a nun (a lovely woman) and we used to visit her in the convent when we were younger. So it wasn't a big shock when I got to secondary school. In Ireland nuns are everywhere (at least they were back then in the mid-70s), part of the fabric of society. Their influence was huge.

I'm not going to identify particular nuns because that would be terribly unfair. It wasn't their fault that they were the way they were. Instead I suppose I blame the system and the stranglehold the Catholic church had on Ireland. And, in fact, of the nuns attached to my school, there was at least one who was a sweetie. However (without giving any clues to her identity) there was one particular nun who really had it in for me. She hovered like a vulture, on the lookout for 'bold lassies' and she was never happier than when she had someone to belittle. Looking back now I can see her more as a human being, perhaps one who was very angry at how her life had turned out, or who was afraid she'd made the wrong choice. But whatever her reasons, the way she brought people to heel (me anyway!) was by humiliating them, rather than imparting kindness and wisdom.

I remember one time when I was about 12 or 13 and my friend and I were at that stage where girls dress similarly. We were both wearing velvet ribbons and this particular nun grabbed us and shrieked, 'Who's the ape? Who's the ape?' over and over again. (She meant, 'Who's copying who?')

She was practically dancing around, pointing her finger and I remember thinking, 'It's as if she's the same age as *us*.' In fact she probably wasn't that much older – and certainly not emotionally. Also, I realise that the nuns wouldn't have been allowed to argue with each other. Instead if they were angry they'd have to go away and pray about it – hardly healthy behaviour. Nowadays, reasonable confrontation is considered a good thing, people learn from it they grow and move on, but back then the prevailing ethos was suppression. Push it down, deny your truth, swallow your anger – and pray about it.

Some years later when I was 16, the local boys' school, The 'Christian' Brothers were holding a disco, but decided that the girls from our school could only go if the nuns okayed it. Realising I had no choice, I approached this same nun and asked her to do the needful and to my great surprise she said she would. The following day in assembly she announced the disco and told everyone to see me for details. 'There,' she said to me afterwards, 'I did what you asked.'

Something about the sly set of her mouth alerted me and anxiously I asked if she'd told the head brother that we were allowed to attend. An expression of the biggest, fakest surprise appeared on her face – 'But why would I do that? When Ye're not allowed to attend.'

Not only had she refused to do something that would have been terribly easy for her but she dropped me in it by making the announcement: I had to spend the next three days explaining to disgruntled wannabe revellers that although there was a disco, we couldn't go. A child of four wouldn't have been so spiteful. Oddly enough, my mother said recently a propos this woman, 'Her bark was worse than her bite.' I'm afraid I have to disagree: she was a piece of work.

There are a lot of robust people who came through the convent system and it didn't take a lump out of them, but I think if you were in any way sensitive or a bit more fragile, as I was, the nuns had the capacity to do enormous damage. A lot of people became *like* the nuns, they used them as their role models and if they read my litany of woe they will probably have no clue what I'm talking about. But, in my opinion, the nuns were just not qualified to be in charge of vulnerable, malleable human beings at that very formative time of their lives. I don't hate them but I have a lot of contempt for them, even now. Catholicism was something that was so deeply ingrained in me that it was a very long time before I could see it as just a collection of superstitions. I remember on one occasion one of the nuns brought in a long carpenter's nail, so we could 'experience' the Crucifixion. The terrible relish with which she went on about it ... 'Oh, imagine it girls, six inch nails through your hands, look at it girls, look at your hands!' Absolutely loving it!

I find the iconography of Catholicism very odd. I'm staggered that there is an image of man on a cross being tortured which we're expected to kneel before. If the image was changed only slightly to that of a man with his fingernails being pulled out by pliers, how comfortable would people be kneeling before that? As for the idea that we are expected to eat this man's body and drink his blood! The nuns used to chuckle at 'People in Darkest Africa' and their arcane blood sacrifices or the Incas and their propensity for flinging virgins off cliffs – but frankly I fail to see the difference. Now, the bloodthirstiness of Catholicism seems sick and bizarre to me, but for years I was simply too close to it to see it objectively.

Tony, my husband, is an atheist and I'm strongly opposed to organised religion. However, that doesn't mean that I don't try to treat people with kindness. I like to think I live my life with a Christian sensibility but I would never describe myself as a Christian. The word retains horrible connotations for me and the more time goes on and the further I get away from my convent days, the more it appals me. But I do think the idea of doing unto others as you would be done by is a wonderful way to live your life.

I learned about sex from my parents and of course in those days everything was couched '*within* marriage' – no such thing as sex any other way. I think we dealt with it (with a lay teacher) in biology but one particular nun, for her own reasons, suddenly decided in the middle of Religious Education that it was vitally important for us to know where our pubic bone was. She started rubbing hers in front of us – it was horrific! Then she starting crying out, 'Feel yours, feel yours, girls!' We were mortified. There was a lot of appalled giggling because we couldn't actually believe that she was making such a show of herself. In retrospect there was a lot more going on there than we knew and it doesn't bear thinking about . . .

I was told that when I began my relationship with alcohol, my emotional development stopped, that even though I was going through the motions of living, I had side-stepped any emotional interaction with life. And until I stopped drinking at the age of thirty, I didn't mature any further. Ironically, I do feel there are similarities between some of the nuns and me: they also opted out of life, simply via a different route and were also somewhat 'emotionally fossilised'.

One of the fundamental tenets of Catholics is that we're born bad. We start life at a spiritual disadvantage; even before we've drawn our first breath we're stained with original sin and burdened with all kinds of horrible visceral urges that the nuns felt it was their duty to suppress and keep in line. Nowadays we nurture young people and try to find the best in children. We say, 'Well, so-and-so isn't academically gifted but he has a wonderful way with people, or he's good at sport.' Or whatever. But back then there was no such thing as trying to find the best in someone – quite the opposite. It was about hunting down any latent badness and banishing it with fear and humiliation. There was never any attempt at recognising the 'whole' person or a human being's uniqueness.

I was academically bright and worked hard but my quirkiness was regarded with horror. The nuns certainly never encouraged me to write – I might have ended up with a glimmer of self-esteem and that would never do! Nothing outside of their rigid by-rote set of goals was encouraged. Maybe it was as well I didn't attempt writing back then because they would have killed any tiny bud of confidence stone dead. My English teacher was a lay teacher and she was encouraging, as was my history teacher (also a lay teacher). I think the ratio of lay teachers to nuns was about 3 to 1 – but the nuns certainly punched above their weight in terms of their influence.

I had a friend who, at the age of about fifteen, went to one of the nuns for career guidance. She said she wanted to go to Trinity College (one of the universities in Dublin). In silence, the nun watched her for a long time, then closed her files and said tartly, 'You'll never go to Trinity, you'll never make anything of yourself.' In fact my friend went on to get her degree and now she has an excellent job in IT. She told me that even at the time she knew that the nun wanted to devastate her. 'She wanted me to start roaring crying. Then I would be "one of them" and they could remould me in whatever way they wanted.' I agree. I truly believe that their gameplan (whether articulated amongst themselves or not) was to try to break us down and then to reconstruct us in their image. As a result, undermining us was their principal weapon.

Since I've been published I've never heard a word from my old school. A friend who had been at school with me said to me recently, 'Wouldn't you think they'd get in touch?' But, not a word. Actually, it was quite funny – I have a lot of German, French and Spanish editions of my books and I sent a selection to the school for their senior language pupils because I thought they might find them helpful. I'm still waiting for my thank you letter!

I do take responsibility for the fact that I was not robust, that I was extra sensitive and difficult at school. I found – and still find – that authority is like a red rag to a bull to me which I acknowledge as very immature. And I don't deny that I silently sent those women strong signals that they were not going to break me down.

I have wondered what my life would have been like if I

had gone to a school where somebody had seen that I was finding it tougher than other people, that I had talents which weren't mainstream, if I had been encouraged rather than scorned. I do think things would have been less unbearable. However, although I took the scenic route to happiness, my life has turned out fine. Maybe it was necessary to carry all that pain, but maybe it would have gone away sooner? Or looking at it another way, maybe if I'd gone to a more progressive compassionate school, I'd just have found something else to be miserable about. Maybe if I'd gone to a mixed school with boys I'd have had my humiliation in another way? Let's face it, I would never have been a cheerleader!

I am sometimes sad about those wasted years but I do try to be forgiving and to remember they didn't know any better. They were just like adolescent girls, with all the bitchiness that goes along with being that age.

Tony and I decided that if we had children there was no way we'd send them to a religious school because I think it just messes people up – if they have the potential to be messed up.

Of the people I know who have young children, some have started going to Mass and sucking up to the local priest in an attempt to get their children into a Catholic school. I think it's partly because it's hard to get children into schools and maybe it's because other schools are regarded as rougher? I don't really know. Whatever, it's their business and I will admit that my attitudes are more extreme than my friends'.

It's taken me a long time to have the courage to speak as

I am now. There was that lingering terror of being con-
demned as 'a bold, bold lassie' or that people would wag
their finger at me. (As I'm sure they will.) But despite their
attempts to convert me into a craven automaton my fear of
the nuns has gone. I realise that despite my best efforts to
protect their identities, by telling my story and agreeing to it
being published, I can be regarded as being cruel. These
women have been given no opportunity to defend themselves or to tell their side of the story and I'm not sure if the
fact that all the ones I've referred to are now dead, makes it
better or worse. But this is my truth. And it's not just a personal truth, it's the truth about a system that was unjust and
imperfect and – yes – cruel. And which, hopefully, won't be
repeated.

I'm sorry that I wasn't able to tell a, 'Hey, we didn't
always see eye-to-eye but at the end of the day the nuns and
I came to respect each other' type of story, but I'm sure
someone else will tell it for me. And as regards the damage
done to me, let's keep it in perspective. I experienced no
physical cruelty – the damage done to me was merely psychological, emotional and spiritual. My experience is
nothing like that of those poor unfortunate girls who had to
endure the industrial schools or Magdalen laundries, where
the nuns were truly savage. Now that so much has come to
light about their sadism I can see that I got off quite lightly.

Sandi Toksvig

Sandi Toksvig was born in Copenhagen, Denmark in 1959. As her father was a foreign correspondent for Danish television she attended several schools, the first being l'Institution de l'Ascension in Copenhagen. She later went to others in Europe, Africa and the United States before going to Girton College, Cambridge University, where she studied law, archaeology and anthropology and graduated with a first class degree in law.

She worked on various theatrical productions before turning to children's television and then the comedy circuit, radio and mainstream television. She has also written a number of novels and children's books.

Sandi has three children and lives in Surrey with her partner Alice.

'When I was about six I would lie in the crucifixion shape, on my stomach, on the stone cold floor of the church. My mother said then she knew what I was going to be – and it wasn't a nun. It was a drama queen!'

I went to lots of different schools but the very first one was a convent. I was there from when I was four until I was eight. It was a Belgian French convent in Copenhagen. Children in Denmark don't normally start school until they're seven but when I reached four I was desperate to go to school. I remember it was a most magnificent building. The nuns there had the full habit, down to the floor, with the veil and the white thing and much clanking of rosaries. They always walked with their hands tucked in their habits, over their chests. It was all very non-Vatican II. I remember I was taken off for a walk in the gardens by Mère Marie Colette to see if I was ready for school. When I was told I was ready I was *thrilled*.

I remember the convent was a rather dark and austere place with very high ceilings and it took me quite a long time to get used to calling everybody 'Mère', because it was a partly French/partly English school, which was strange in Copenhagen. It was a real United Nations of kids, lots of American kids, Jews, Arabs, Protestants, kids from all over.

I remember a new woman turned up and I think she partly took over. She was called Mother Bernadette and it seemed even more bizarre to call her 'Mother'. I thought that was hilarious, with her being a nun. Unusually for that time, all the children were dropped off at the school so if you were late it was never going to be your fault, it was always going to be your parents' fault. Yet despite this, if you were late, the nuns made you sit on the stairs in the dark and I remember that to this day as odd. I began to develop a sense of injustice. I thought 'wait a minute, it's not my fault – let my Dad sit on the stairs instead – it's not in my hands that I'm late'.

I also began to realise the nuns whom I had thought were such a pious lot were not in fact very nice. Such a lot of bitching went on. And the convent was not quite what I had imagined it to be. A place of incredible piety and kindness? It certainly was not. It was a mix of terror and an endless sense of darkness. The nuns were very strict and I remember sitting with my hands on top of the desk at all times. The two I remember most clearly were particularly strict: Mother Bernadette and Mère Nicolette, two pinched-faced women with glasses on the end of their noses. I don't remember any affection, any warmth – indeed I don't recall them taking any pleasure in the fact they were dealing with little children all day. Their lives seemed rather dreary and dull. The funny thing is that there is this rebellious bit of me which doesn't want to conform and it brought that out. Early on in my life I felt there was a sense of injustice and I still think like that. I'm a great one for standing up and saying that's not right, that's not fair – and it started there. I didn't like the way children were punished – or how quickly and rapidly they were crushed. It was almost so repressive that you were either going to buckle under completely or stand up and complain – and I turned out to be a complainer.

I think I was nothing but trouble to them because when I was seven I led probably the first and almost certainly only strike they ever had! We were not allowed to go out to play because it had been raining and there were puddles in the playground. I led a general strike of my form because I was furious, enraged. I organised posters and we had a strike then we were allowed to go out to play – so that was a huge success.

I do remember being incredibly impressed with the theatricality of it all though. I liked the idea of the costumes, the idea of devoting your whole life to something. In fact when I was about six, in break times, I used to go and lie on the floor of the church in the position I knew the novices had to lie when they were dedicating themselves to God. I would lie in the crucifixion shape on my stomach on the stone cold floor, just giving myself to God. Obviously I must have gone to one of the ceremonies and seen a novice take her vows, lying on the floor and I just remember finding it very comforting. My mother said then she knew what I was going to be – and it wasn't a nun. It was a drama queen!

Besides the nuns, there were also lay teachers. We had one whom I remember as a child thinking she was *the* most beautiful woman I had ever seen. Just stunning and blonde with the most beautiful hair. The thing I most remember about her is that she could draw *anything* on the blackboard, she was a wonderful artist. But she said goodbye to us at the end of term because she had made the decision to join a closed order of Carmelites. They don't speak, they're completely enclosed – and it just put me off the whole thing *forever*. I thought 'you are *so* beautiful . . .' – this extraordinary blonde woman, this incredible artistic skill – and it seemed to me it was going to go for nothing. She was a great communicator, I remember laughing in her classes and I loved being taught by her. What a terrible waste! How unfair that she was going to go away and devote herself to a life of prayer and I thought it was truly terrible.

My parents certainly weren't Catholics, not remotely, but mother did start working at the school. She taught current affairs to the older girls and as my father was a journalist she was particularly well suited to do that but I think the nuns were rather shocked by some of the information my mother was happy to give out. There was very much a sense of you were not 'of the world' when you were there. You went into an airlock, a strange time capsule with huge, high ceilings where everything was dark. The curious thing is that where we were living, in a small suburb of Copenhagen, in all the years we lived there I never saw any of the nuns anywhere. Not in a shop, in a café or a bank – in places where you generally meet members of the community. You only ever saw them within this very small stage set.

When I was about seven and a half my father was posted to America. Before we left he told the nuns they could have the use of his Fiat 500 for however long we were away. The first thing they said to my mother was 'How long do we have to borrow the car before we get to keep it?' That was their first question, not 'thanks very much'. The school had a most impressive circular drive and at one point, after we'd left, the head nun came to visit from Belgium. All the children were lined up in their little sailor outfits, the traditional

Danish school uniform, to welcome this nun. Eventually four nuns arrived in our old Fiat 500 and as it pulled to a stop the entire bottom of the car fell out and the four nuns were deposited on the spot! They wrote to us in America to tell us what had happened and I remember my father *sobbing* with laughter! They also said we were now responsible for getting rid of the car from the front drive.

We left to go to America in 1966 and at that point none of the Vatican II changes had percolated through. The Mass was still in Latin, the habits were still this heavy thick serge. It was a horrible fabric, you didn't really want to touch it. There were long sleeves and you just saw a small piece of the face – not even a forehead – just a white band across and those long veils.

After that going to America was extraordinary. For a start you didn't wear a uniform and when I went in '67 it was the beginning of flower power and the hippie thing. Some of the teachers encouraged you to call them by their first names. It felt open and light – all quite extraordinary. It was only then I realised how heavy the whole religious thing had been. Starting and ending every lesson with prayers and tributes to the saints. We prayed a lot and I know there was a lot of shutting your eyes and thinking about what you'd done. I'd shut my eyes and think 'I haven't done any-thing, I don't know what the issue is here.' So lots of introspection – but the actual catechism, rotes and things like that I don't recall at all.

I don't think I was adversely affected by any of it, partly because my father was so adamantly against it. He thought it was all a load of old tosh. I don't know if it's still the case but it used to be that if you were born in Denmark, which is a Protestant country, you automatically belonged to the Church. If you didn't want to belong to the Church you had to get a separate Act of Parliament passed to remove yourself from the Church. Then you didn't have to pay tax towards the upkeep of the Church. My father actually bothered to do that (and it was the Devil's own trouble when we wanted to bury him but that was later). However, there is no way that he would have sent me there if he'd thought I was going to get a religious education. One thing did surprise me though. Years and years later he met the present Pope and said it was an extraordinary experience and that he believed him to be a good man. He said he was surprisingly moved by the meeting. I think the present Pope is one of the most reactionary and appallingly backward-looking people that the Church has ever been led by so I'm surprised. I can only assume that the man has a lot of personal magnetism which doesn't come across to me. I think the fact I left when I was seven and a half is a good thing. I think it hadn't been so sufficiently drummed into me. All I knew was that the very regulated, very strict way of life didn't really suit me.

I did love the music and I'm still a sucker for Catholic iconography. I absolutely love the colour, the bells and the smells. To this day I love ritual and although I'm not religious I'm very happy to go to church services. I like the standing up, the sitting down, repeating things by rote. I like the whole sense of belongingness, being in a community and the sense of some kind of spiritual thing happening. I certainly don't associate convent life with any spiritual happening, which is a shame. I've got a friend who was brought

up a Catholic and she says the main thing she got out of it
was that she knows the names of all the saints who died in
hideous circumstances. The ones who were crushed to
death or died in a very unpleasant manner. I have a daily
radio show and to this day I name the patron saint which is
a sort of nod in the direction of the old nuns. What I can't
quite believe is that there is a patron saint for *everything*. I've
not found a subject yet that does not have a patron saint.
There's one for travel hostesses and what I like is they've all
got different aliases and many different names. There's a
patron saint of weavers, called something very bizarre but
known to his friends as Humphrey, Humphrey the Hermit.

My children go to State schools. I'm not in favour of private education although I'm very fortunate in that it's a very
easy decision for me to make because the area we live in has
extremely good schools. I'm also a very committed parent so
if the school needs something, if there's a gap, I'm very
happy to help – organise other parents or go along or whatever it takes, so that everybody benefits. That's my brand of
socialism, for everybody. But I do know a couple of people
who have sent their children to very good local Catholic
schools, not because they're Catholic but because it provides a very good and strict education.

I've certainly never regretted going to school so early. I've
revelled all my life in being surrounded by books. I'm never
more comfortable than sitting in a library and my choice, if
I could do anything, would be to go back to learning full-
time. I just have a thirst for it.

My neighbour's sister is a nun and I've met her on several
occasions. You'd never know it from the way she dresses – in

comfortable, casual clothes, like everyone else. It's nothing like what I knew. In fact I still have an obsession with the whole nun thing. I'm writing a new musical with Dilly Kean from Fascinating Aida and it's going to be about nuns. It's definitely going to have the traditional 'proper black and white thing'. So yes, I still retain an endless fascination with nuns. In my bathroom at home I buy those Catholic candles with pictures of the saints on. There's something, a resonance of it that stays with me and the convent left me with strong feelings about injustice – that's a good thing.

Selected Bibliography

Anderson, Bonnie S. and Zinsser, Judith P., *A History of Their Own: Women in Europe from Prehistory to the Present Vol. I & II*, Penguin, 1988

Binchy, Maeve, *Light a Penny Candle*, Coronet edition, 1983 (First published 1982)

Boylan, Clare, *Concerning Virgins*, Penguin, 1990 (First published 1989)

Boyle, Katie, *What This Katie Did*, Sphere Books, 1982 (First published 1980)

Chitty, Susan (ed). *As Once in May: the Early Autobiography of Antonia White*, Virago Press, 1983

Devlin, Polly, *All of Us There*, Pan Books, 1988 (First published 1984)

Donnelly, Frances, *Shake Down the Stars*, Corgi, 1990 (First published 1988)

Fell, Christine, *Women in Anglo-Saxon England*, Blackwell, 1986 (First published 1984)

Flannery, Austin, *Vatican Council II Vols 1 & 2*, Dominican Publications, 1987 (First published 1975)

Fraser, Antonia, *The Weaker Vessel: Woman's Lot in Seventeenth Century England*, Mandarin, 1989 (First published 1984)

Grace, Gerald, *Catholic Schools, Mission, Markets and Morality*, Routledge, 2002

Greer, Germaine, *The Female Eunuch*, Paladin, 1989 (First published 1970)

Moorman, J.H.R., *A History of the Church in England*, Third edition, A & C Black, 1980

Orchard, M. Emmanuel, *Till God Will*, Darton, Longman and Todd, 1985

O'Malley, Mary, *Once a Catholic*, Amber Lane Press, 1978

Usherwood, Elizabeth, *Women First: Biographies of Catholic Women in the Forefront of Change*, Sheed & Ward, 1989

Walsh, John, *Growing Up Catholic*, Papermac, 1989

Warner, Marina, *Alone of All Her Sex: The Myth and the Cult of the Virgin Mary*, Picador, 1990 (First published 1976)

White, Antonia, *Frost in May*, Virago Modern Classics, 1978 (First published 1933)